JAMES STONE

THE
TRAEGER
GRILL BIBLE
2023

2000 Days of Smoke & Delicious Traeger Recipes for Beginners and Advanced Users | Become the Undisputed Grill Master of Your Neighborhood

Table
of content

Chapter 3
Meat-Based Recipes 37

Chapter 4
Vegetable-Based Recipes 52

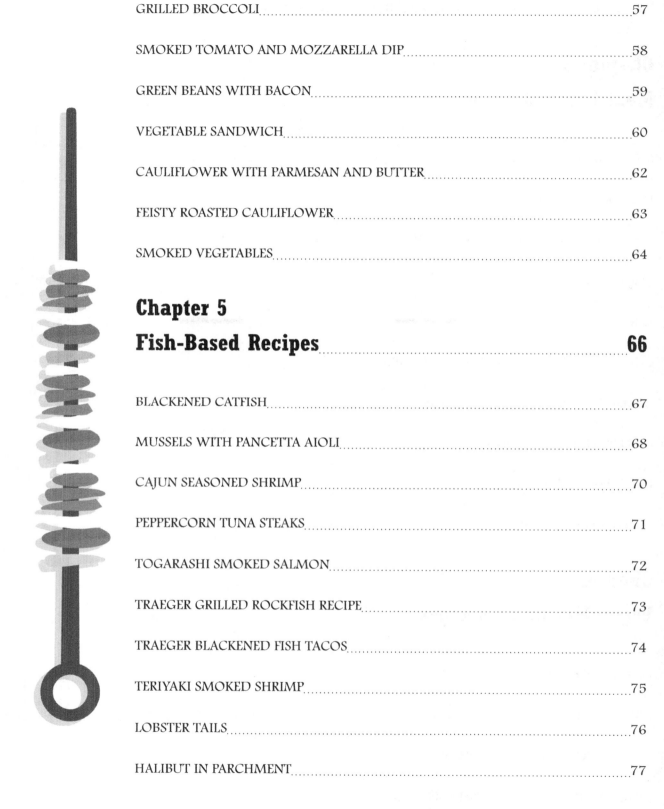

Chapter 5
Fish-Based Recipes

Chapter 6
Soups and Snacks Recipes 79

Chapter 7
Desserts Recipes 95

Introduction

Congrats! You just purchased the finest grill you will ever get. But what precautions must you take to ensure it becomes the only grill you ever need? Although the Traeger grills are durable equipment, proper usage, care, and cleaning will enable them to perform well for years to come and give hours of pleasurable family meals, free from worrying about unpleasant aromas and inconvenient malfunctions.

Many smokers begin by learning how to use upright charcoal smokers. These practical, affordable equipment compel you to get the knowledge necessary to correctly smoke various types of meat. The temperature management and venting need a lot of experience.

However, you'll suddenly have a different experience after getting a Traeger Grill. The high-tech features of Traeger Grills eliminate a lot of the guesswork and make smoking simpler. Using a Traeger will change the way you see smoking forever.

Consider this your comprehensive reference to everything you need to know about Traeger Grills, including how they operate, what makes certain models costlier than others, and how to use one to obtain the greatest smoked meat of your life. A Traeger is a wise purchase when you're looking for the least frustrating method to smoke meat, cheese, or veggies.

It uses an auger to move pellets from a side-mounted hopper into the center burn chamber, where they are lit by a hot metal rod. You must plug it in since those systems need the power to function. It has

integrated meat thermometers and accurate, digital temperature control. All you have to do to use it is put pellets in the hopper, switch it on, and choose the desired temperature—anything from "smoke" to 450 degrees Fahrenheit.

Chapter 1
Traeger Grill:
An Introduction

1.1 The Fundamentals of Wood Pellet

Real barbecue may be challenging since it requires a lot of care, time, and effort in addition to hot, unclean coals and a potentially hazardous fire. However, the payoff for the effort is in the outcomes. Without low temperatures, some time, and high-quality hardwood smoke, it is impossible to produce succulent and flavorful meals that have been smoked. Although untidy, charcoal briquettes are acceptable. While big log-burning barbecues are overkill for the majority of patios, hardwood logs are wonderful for barbecue purists. Barbecue is now simpler thanks to wood pellet fuel. The small pellets are simple to handle and burn similarly to logs, yet they produce very little ash.

Modern wood pellet grills provide all the comfort of electric smokers with a few extra advantages, such as the ability to cook food at higher temperatures, the use of real wood to generate the cooking heat, and the absence of soot or wasted fuel due to the pellets' lack of moisture, which is present in green or wet wood.

Controlling the cook is your responsibility as the pit master. With a nice pellet smoker, your life will be a little bit simpler, but there are still a few factors to which you'll want to pay particular attention.

The following are the six factors for grilling and smoking using wood pellets:

1. Time: You should give the amount of time you will require additional consideration and preparation, from preheating to reclining the meat rest after a cook. The majority of wood pellet grills have a crucial warmup window to follow. Cooking times may be prolonged when using bigger chunks of meat and low and slow cooking. Start early and allow enough time for adjustments so you can finish by the desired serving time. Large pieces of meat should be given an additional 10-minute "rest" after being removed from the grill before being carved.

2. The meat: Your "cooking" adventure begins at the grocery store or butcher counter, where you choose the best-looking slices. The best-tasting meats are higher-quality cuts with greater fat. Always remember that larger pieces need longer cooking times and add spice.

3. Spices: The recipes in this book have wonderful seasoning combinations outlined. Use the best spices you can find since freshness makes a difference. Spices may also be "bloomed" to release oils and intensify tastes in a dry frying pan at low heat.

4. Smoke type: Pick a wood pellet taste that goes with the meat. The consistency of these recipes depends on the wood you pick.

5. Placement: The convection-like heat circulation created by the fan and the heat deflector gives your wood pellet grill a highly consistent cooking temperature without the normal hot spots. Still,

try to place your meal in the smoke's path as it enters the chamber.

6. Temperature: Smoking at lower cook temperatures allows the meat to absorb the most smoke flavor while breaking down the collagen and fat in the meat. Cooking time and temperature may also be impacted by the outside temperature. Try to place your wood pellet barbecue away from strong, direct winds.

Just a few more temperature-related hints...

Creating hot and cool "zones" on traditional grills where you may move meats to regulate cooking times is advised. On wood pellet grills, such a strategy is not an option. Alternatively, you'll work with predetermined heat settings, including hot smoking, cool smoking, and smoke roasting.

Most low-and-slow beef smoking occurs between 225°F and 275°F. Traditional smoking occurs at lower temperatures. The actual magic takes place when the temperature is this low. Low-temperature meats are slowly enticed into fall-off-the-bone succulence with this set-it-and-forget-it form of wood pellet cooking.

However, cooking at reduced temperatures won't always prevent you from overcooking your meal. Foods should be cooked to a range of internal temperatures. For instance, leaner meat cuts are more likely to dry out. You'll get jerky if you're not cautious!

The simplest way to explain using the wood pellet grill at higher temperatures is to smoke roast. You'll get high-heat char and browning, much as on a gas grill, but you'll also receive smoke flavor. On a Trager, you can do the majority of baking and culinary tasks that you can perform in your home oven.

All Trager's well-known wood pellet grill smokers have a maximum temperature above 400°F.

Although they are equally simple to use, electric smokers only reach a maximum temperature of 275°F. They lack nearly as much versatility.

When we come to the recipes, we'll slip in a few specialties that benefit from high heat, like reverse searing, because the pellet grill can reach greater temperatures than a standard smoker.

1.2 Types of Traeger Grill

1.2.1 PELLET GRILLS

Like those offered by Traeger, a pellet grill uses hardwood pellets to heat and flavor meals. In contrast to charcoal or gas grills, wood pellet grills don't use an open flame for cooking food. Rather, indirect heat and smoke are used for cooking meals on pellet grills. When using indirect heat, food cooks uniformly without the need to move the chicken about to prevent hoteaspoonots and flare-ups.

BEST GRILLING FOODS

Smoked meats, for example, brisket or pulled pork, are some of the most well-liked dishes to prepare on a pellet barbecue. But because a pellet grill works like an oven, you are not restricted to cooking BBQ. You can cook casseroles, desserts, steaks, and sides on a pellet grill. A pellet grill may even be used to make bread.

GRILL AND FUEL PRICES

You may spend from $500 to $2000 on a pellet grill. A standard-sized bag of the wood pellets needed to power a pellet barbecue often costs less than $20. (which is the same as a gas tank).

PROS AND CONS

Benefits: Pellet grills are a flexible cooking appliance. They heat up fast, are simple to adjust for temperature, and cook food evenly while imparting a great smokey taste. Several culinary techniques may be employed with pellet grills, such as smoking, roasting, braising, grilling, and baking. Additionally, you don't need extra care since you can adjust your pellet grill's temperature and walk away.

Cons: Because pellet grills need power, bringing them camping or to the beach might be challenging unless you have an inverter or generator. Some claim that a pellet grill cannot produce a decent sear, but this is untrue. Traeger wood pellet grills can achieve temperatures of 500 degrees, so you can obtain a standard or reverse seal.

1.2.2 CHARCOAL GRILLS

Charcoal is the fuel source for a charcoal barbecue. It is well-liked for its mobility and typical cheap price. However, it has a few drawbacks, such as the potential for flare-ups, uneven cooking, and lengthy warm-up periods.

BEST GRILLING FOODS

The most popular foods to barbecue over charcoal are hot dogs, chicken, and hamburgers.

GRILL AND FUEL PRICES

The average price of a charcoal barbecue is roughly $100, although heavy-duty ones may cost up to hundreds of dollars. A 20-pound package of charcoal briquettes or lumps usually costs approximately $20.

CHARCOAL GRILL TYPES

Barrel, kettle, and ceramic kamado grills are the three most popular kinds of charcoal barbecues.

PROS AND CONS

Benefits: Charcoal grills are inexpensive, have a convenient fuel supply, and are simple to locate in shops.

Cons: Since charcoal grills naturally have cold and hot patches in the grill, they take longer to heat up, are more likely to cause flare-ups, and make it harder to cook your food evenly.

1.2.3 GAS GRILLS

A backyard staple is gas barbecues, often known as propane grills. As the name suggests, they use propane as their fuel, which is delivered to the grill by a propane tank.

BEST GRILLING FOODS

Hot dogs and hamburgers, among other meals, cook nicely on gas barbecues. They're also well-known for hearty veggies like squash and portobello mushrooms. Gas grills perform best when you don't need to or want to add flavor while cooking. This is because, unlike a pellet or charcoal grill, gas does not add additional taste to meals.

GRILL AND FUEL PRICES

Depending on the manufacturer and its amenities, a gas barbecue may cost anywhere from a little over $100 to over $1000. The price of a 20-pound propane grill tank varies based on the propane price but is often between $20 and $30.

PROS AND CONS

Benefits: Gas grills are inexpensive, simple to operate, and rapidly reach high temperatures.

Cons: Unlike charcoal or pellet grills, food cooked on a gas grill doesn't have a smokey taste. They may also catch fire if food fat comes into contact with the grill's open flames.

1.2.4 PORTABLE GRILLS

A broad range of forms and fuel sources are available for portable barbecues. Portable charcoal grills, portable wood pellet grills and portable gas grills are all available. Many are excellent for camping. Some are more suited for a tailgate or a trip to the beach.

BEST GRILLING FOODS

Since portable grills are smaller by design, hot dogs, hamburgers, and veggies are the most common foods to cook on them. Some portable barbecues, however, have the capacity to cook a spatchcocked chicken or an entire rack of ribs.

GRILL AND FUEL PRICES

The fuel source and brand of a portable barbecue affect its price. It is possible to get a portable charcoal barbecue for less money and a very tiny portable gas grill for as low as $50. Modern portable pellet grills provide a more consistent cooking experience. Because of this, their starting price is in the low hundreds.

PORTABLE GRILL TYPES

Portable charcoal barbecues, propane grills or portable gas, and portable wood pellet smokers or grills are several kinds of portable grills.

PROS AND CONS

Benefits: Traveling grilling is made easy with portable barbecues. They'll feed friends and family during tailgates, picnics, beach parties, and camping excursions.

Cons: You have less room since portable grills can only cook a small amount of food once compared to a standard-sized grill.

1.2.5 BBQ SMOKERS

A grill that uses indirect heat to smoke meat is a barbecue smoker. One sort of smoker is a pellet grill. The ideal technique to cook pig and brisket is in barbecue smokers, which gently cook meals at moderate temperatures.

BEST GRILLING FOODS

Pulled pork, chicken and brisket are among the barbecue meats that smokers most often use.

GRILL AND FUEL PRICES

Different smokers spend different amounts of money and use various kinds of fuel. Due to its ability to naturally impart a smokey taste to food, consumer-grade smokers often prefer wood pellets. Small charcoal smokers might be purchased for less than $100. Costs for premium pellet grills might reach $2000.

VARIOUS KINDS OF SMOKERS

There are six basic kinds of barbecue smokers: kamado barbecues, vertical water smokers, offset smokers, wood pellet grills, box smokers (also known as vault smokers), and drum smokers. The majority of non-commercial grill masters like smokers with a pellet or kamado grill.

OFFSET SMOKER

PROS AND CONS

Benefits: Smokers for barbecue provide succulent brisket, pulled pork, and poultry. There are no open flames, and the meat is cooked evenly over a lengthy time.

Cons: Food takes longer to cook, and barbecue smokers may be pricey. It takes more study to learn how to utilize a BBQ smoker than to fire up a grill. Maintaining a uniform and stable temperature when cooking with wood requires maneuvering and management.

1.3 Why Choose a Wood Pellet Smoker and Grill?

A wood pellet smoker offers ease and adaptability, which we've previously discussed, but it also produces the best-tasting, moistest food you've ever tasted. I'm not making this up. Additionally, operating and maintaining your smoker is simple. To get started cooking, all you need to do is help ensure the hopper is stocked with wood pellets and that it is hooked into a power source. With other smoker grills, you'll need to keep an eye on the appliance to maintain the temperature. Once you have a wood pellet grill or smoker, you don't need to do this since they are particularly designed to keep the temperature within certain ranges.

One of its best features is the wood pellet smoker and grill's capacity to keep a temperature low enough to produce the most flavorful smoke. The general agreement is that the meat's surface temperature should be below 140 Fahrenheit to smoke protein, which is simple to do with a wood pellet smoker.

Wood pellet grills' fuel efficiency is also important to note. You may convert your wood pellet griller into an outdoor convection oven by turning on the fan, which reduces the number of wood chips you need to use compared to charcoal or gas grills.

Last but not least, the simplicity of cleaning a wood pellet grill was a major selling feature. After a family BBQ, you don't want to spend much time cleaning. The wood pellet grill doesn't need to empty the firepot after each use; cleaning is simple.

1.4 Advantages of Traeger Grill

There are numerous benefits to utilizing "The Original Traeger Grill", but some things stand out as the qualities that set it apart from other gas or charcoal grills.

1. The Fuel is first and foremost! All other barbecues run on either natural gas, charcoal, or propane. All grills that utilize one of these as fuel necessitate that the user has an extensive understanding of their grill and are often required to be there to "babysit" the grill. Wood pellets made entirely of natural wood are used in Traeger grills! These pellets provide excellent convenience, assurance, and taste while burning in a regulated system. All Natural Traeger Wood Pellets are FDA authorized, suitable for use in restaurants, and available in 11 varieties (all other fuels are available in one flavor). Combined, these pellets may provide hundreds of tastes unique to each user. When burning, these pellets offer a wonderful perfume to every community of Traeger Owners in America, with no negative environmental effects!!

2. With the 3 Speed Smoker Control or the upgraded digital thermostat adjustment, true temperature control is possible in cold, moderate, or hot conditions. Because of the Traeger Grill's regular cook times and the almost nonexistent chance of food burning, the user is able to cook with assurance on the lower-midrange and high settings. It is a reliable outdoor cooking tool. On the Traeger, you can even bake biscuits and pizza with this degree of temperature control!

3. Induction of Air Only Traeger Grills is the ONLY True WOOD PELLET GRILLS with a 4" Induction Fan, which circulates the hot, smoke-filled air around the meal while feeding the burning pellets the air they need to burn hot and effectively. You do not need to move your meat around the heat since the Traeger Grill transfers the heat around the meat! Convection-style cooking It is incredibly simple and productive to smoke, bake, roast, and grill outside with this air induction method since the grill may be "sealed" below.

4. A SYSTEM FOR MANAGING GREASE A Grease Management System (GMS) is a feature that is included on every Traeger grill. When coated with foil, a slanted grease tray transfers the grease from the grill into a bucket and makes cleaning simple by preventing "Old Grease" from building up within the grill. Additionally, this GMS prevents flare-ups that result in damaged food, grill damage, and uncontrollable cooking temperatures.

5. Safety. The firepot includes a drip pan and a stainless-steel diffuser covering its whole stainless body. The likelihood of creating any breakages is relatively low as long as you keep minimum cleaning. Grills that use pellets do not have an open flame. The likelihood of flare-ups and grease fires rises while cooking directly over the fire. As a result, the pellet grill is among the safest tools for outdoor cooking.

6. Flexibility. Because you can carefully regulate the temperature, which varies from roughly 180 to 500 degrees, the pellet grill is significant. A temperature control mechanism on the high-tech pellet grills enables a long, leisurely cook. With a pellet smoker, you are allowed to smoke, roast, and grill. Direct grilling is an option on certain pellet barbecues, which are more adaptable than most other grilling methods.

7. Simple to Use. Pellet grills come with a number of features that make cooking simple. They start with straightforward controls that are simple to learn. Some skill is needed to get the meat to perfection on other grills and smokers, such as charcoal smokers. Commercially scented hardwood pellets are used in pellet grills, and the smoke is milder than with traditional wood pieces.

8. Speedy Cooking. Utilizing firewood and smokers to cook meals more quickly is becoming quite popular. Pellet grills may help you cook meals more quickly and easily while also saving you time. They can quickly warm in only 10 minutes, which is much less time than other barbeque grills. Once again, they have the capacity to hold heat for a long time.

9. A variety. It would be advisable to attempt cooking with firewood pellet smokers and grills, even if you're a newbie. For the culinary specialists, they come in a variety of sizes and shapes. The demands and desires of consumers for practical cooking instruments are considered while manufacturing pellet grills. These grills' pellets come in various tastes, including maple, apple, and hickory, making

them perfect for specialty barbecue shops.

10. Excellent Flavor. The taste and quality of the food produced on a pellet grill are two of its main benefits. Because wood offers superior BBQ spices, renowned professional barbecue cooks utilize it. In contrast to charcoal, you may alter the taste by selecting a different kind of wood pellet. You can cook meals quicker and with less smoke with a pellet grill. They're excellent for those who like spending time with their family since you can set the grills without always watching them. A pellet grill is necessary and beneficial for a fantastic experience if you like smoking or grilling meals.

Chapter 2
Mastering Your Traeger Grill

You need to know a few things to get the most out of your Traeger grill before we can get on to the fun part, which is the recipes. In this chapter, let's examine the various methods and cooking advice you might need.

You have choices thanks to the adaptability of a pellet grill or smoker. Fewer grills on the market provide you with as many options for smoking food. Learning these skills can help you cook outdoors on days when you don't want to heat the house or dirty your spotless stove, in addition to making you look beautiful in front of friends and family.

2.1 Maintaining Your Traeger Grill

Understanding how to properly clean and maintain your Traeger grill is essential.

Why not make sure that your barbecue performs properly for many years because you made the wise decision to get one that will last a lifetime?

You must understand the major parts of your Traeger grills in order to maintain them. Even if you are not an expert at DIY projects and are more likely to contact a repair agency if there is a problem, you still need to understand how your grill is constructed, if only to properly clean it. The machine comprises eight primary parts that work together to give you outcomes you won't get from any other grill.

The following is a list of the key elements:

HARDWOOD PALLETS

The grill's most crucial component is the hardwood pellets. They serve as the grill's primary fuel source. While cooking through them, natural hardwood flavorings may bleed into your dish. Any kind of wood may be used to give your food a unique flavor.

HOPPER

You should place your wood pellets here. Here, when the wood burns and the meal cooks, seasoning takes place. 100% wood, no need for a gas or charcoal hookup.

CONTROLLER

The knob enables you to select your preferred temperature and control it while cooking.

THE INDUCTION FAN

A fan activates as you turn on the grill, heating the food evenly while using the convection cooking method. Hot air is delivered evenly around the grill thanks to the Fan.

AUGER

It is a tool that resembles a screw that picks up and drops the wood pellets into the firepot to ignite them.

A HOT ROD

This is where the fire meets the pellets and ignites. It is at the drill's tip.

FIREPOT

Fire is activated automatically, igniting the hotrod and setting the pellets on fire.

DRIP TRAY

This metal shields the grill from the flames, lessening food charring. It permits the passage of heat and smoke.

HOW DOES IT WORK?

The auger receives the wood pellets from the hopper. More wood pellets are put into the drill to accommodate greater temperatures. The drill then moves the wood pallets to the firepot, where a fire is already blazing. The hotrod ignites the piece of wood when it is placed in the firepot, resulting in smoke and fire discharge. To put out the open flame, a drip tray sits perfectly on top of the burning wood and the hotrod. When the device's internal fan is activated, the food on the grill's top receives an equal distribution of heat and smoke. Some grills now come with an app that allows the chef to precisely set the temperature to suit his or her requirements.

The Traeger wood pallet barbecue may be used for roasting, smoking, baking, braising and grilling.

HOW TO CLEAR THE TRAEGER:

To maintain your grill's authentic, wood-fired taste, it is essential to keep it clean and clear of accumulated grease and debris. The easiest method is to give your barbecue routine cleanings and maintenance.

NOTE: Ensure your grill is unplugged from the socket and shut off.

The following things should be close at hand:

◊ Grill grates made of wood may be cleaned of grease. Trager markets Traeger All-Natural Grease Cleaner; however, regular kitchen grease cleaner will function just as well. Even better, if you clean it often, you may want to think about using a spray bottle with vinegar or lemon juice that has been diluted with water (at a 60 percent concentration).

◊ Bucket Liners

◊ Disposable Gloves

◊ Drip Tray Liners

◊ Shop Vac

◊ Bottle Brush

◊ Paper Towels

Following are the steps to follow:

1. Spray the grease cleanser on the grates.

2. Spray the interior of the chimney

3. Using the wooden grill grate scraper, remove and clean the grates. Instead of using wire brushes, use a cleaning cloth or thick paper towels to dry the grates.

4. Remove the drip tray liner.

5. Remove the drip tray

6. Remove the heat baffle.

7. Vacuum the grill's inside.

8. Use a bottle brush to clean the chimney's inside. Once again, avoid using wire brushes to clean the grates and use a cleaning cloth or thick paper towels.

9. Spray your grease remover on the walls.

10. Allow soaking before wiping with paper towels.

11. Reinstall the heat baffle

12. Reinstall the drip tray

13. Reinstall the drip tray lining.

14. Add a fresh bucket liner.

15. Reinsert the grate

Every time you grill, you don't have to go through the entire procedure since the taste of the meat comes from the previously used charred and impregnated grill grates. However, if you use it regularly, you should do it twice or three times each grilling season. Experts advise cleaning it immediately away if you are cooking anything extremely greasy. If you prevent the fat from congealing, it will make the work much simpler.

Here are some helpful recommendations for regular maintenance to help you prevent issues and make cleaning a little easier:

1. Purchase a cover. The Traeger covers are a tad pricey, but they look nice. If you decide to purchase a Trager cover, be sure to thoroughly cover it with a plastic sheet. You run the danger of water getting into the hopper if you keep your Traeger grill outdoors in rainy weather. The pellets may block your auger if they expand while moist. You cannot cook with damp wood, as well.

2. Regularly replace the foil on the greased pan and clean it. Even if you're tempted to crash after the party, take the time to scrape the excess debris and grease from the grease drain tube and the greased pan and replace the grease pan foil to prevent grease build-up. Grease is simpler to clean while it's still somewhat warm. You run the danger of a grease fire if the drain tube becomes blocked.

3. Clear out the grease container. But the task is straightforward enough: dump the grease into a container you can throw away, like a plastic bottle. Avoid pouring it down the drain or into the gutter! Use hot water and soap to wash the bucket, or line it with aluminum foil that you can throw away to make cleanup simpler.

4. Clean up the surfaces outside. Keep the powder coating brand new since the Trager grills are lovely items! Wipe it with paper towels or a clean cloth after washing it with warm water and soap. Avoid using scouring pads or abrasive cleansers!

5. Remove additional ash from the fire pot, even if you don't want to thoroughly clean it, at least once every five times you use it. To do this, take out the drain pan, the grates, and the heat baffle. For this task, a shop vac may be used. Ensure that the grill is disconnected and not turned on and that all the parts are cool.

2.2 Maintaining Temperature

It could be challenging to maintain a wood pellet grill's temperature.

Traeger's temperature control mechanisms regulate like a champ, even though different wood pellet mixes burn at various speeds and temperatures.

Here are some methods you may take to maintain temperatures if your wood pellet grill has trouble doing so.

Cooking over fire is similar to cooking in a convection oven since interior temperatures may change if the door or lid is opened and heat escapes.

How to keep the temperature inside a Traeger constant:

Traeger temperature controls precisely measure the interior grill temperature and temperature gauges at the moment you see it. When you open it, the temperature inside may fluctuate.

1. Using Traeger pellets is always recommended.

2. Check the dryness of your pellets. Wet or moist pellets may not ignite, burn unevenly, or otherwise perform poorly in your wood-fired barbecue.

3. Keep your grill clean to maintain even temperatures and keep ash out of the firepot to maintain airflow.

The RTD temperature controller should be cleaned. It is adjacent to the hopper on the left side of your grill's interior.

5. Fill your hopper to the brim to ensure you have enough pellets to feed the fire.

6. Change to a newer type of temperature controller. With its Advanced Grilling Logic, the 2016 Digital Pro Temperature Controller monitors the core temperature every 60 seconds and feeds the fire if there are any variations from the predetermined internal temperature. Precision control is ensured by replacing the temperature gauge with this controller.

7. The grill of an older barbecue may be corroded or rusted. If the fire pot has too many holes, you have too much air streaming into the fire, which might lead to variable temperatures. Order a new fire pot or improve your barbecue if this is the situation.

Keep in mind that constant temperatures produce consistently excellent food.

2.3 What Foods Can You Cook on a Pellet Smoker?

You can cook anything on a pellet grill if it can be smoked, roasted, baked (yes, baked), or grilled. The greatest benefit of a pellet grill above most other cookers is perhaps versatility.

The convection method of cooking holds the key. Large pieces of lamb, beef, pork, or entire fowl may be perfectly cooked in that ambient heat. They work well for smaller foods, including steaks, sausages, burgers, chicken wings, and more.

You won't get the sear, but the meal will be perfectly cooked.

Do not forget to include some vegetables. It's hardly hyperbole to say that a pellet grill can prepare a whole dinner.

And save room for dessert before you try cornbread, pizza, or even cookies and brownies! Now you're wondering, "Smokey brownies? Not at all."

Don't worry; pellets burn cleanly and emit less smoke at higher temperatures. No smoke is created after you turn the temperature up to baking.

2.4 Cooking Tips and Tricks

Let's first look at the suggested minimum internal temperatures before discussing the significance of high-quality meat and seasoning. Use a digital food thermometer for cooking all items to these degrees before taking the meat from the heat source for safety. Despite this, heating meals at a higher temperature is not harmful. It all comes down to individual choice.

Chops, steaks, and roasts of beef, lamb, pork, and veal should be cooked to a temperature of 145 degrees Fahrenheit. Meat needs at least three minutes of rest.

None of the cut poultry must be cooked to a temperature of 165 degrees Fahrenheit.

145 degrees Fahrenheit is the ideal temperature for cooking fish and shellfish.

Now that you know the ideal cooking temperature, the quality of the meat and the seasoning should be considered while using a wood pellet grill or smoker. It is advised to compare the quality of many nearby butcher shops before choosing one. Your work will be halfway done if your beef is of good quality.

Second, seasoning has a crucial role. It should blend in with the natural tastes of the dish you're
preparing rather than overpowering the meat. Your meal's "wow factor" may soar to new heights

using the correct spice. You can create your blend of spices and tastes. Just be sure the seasoning you choose is suitable for low-and-smoking and slow cooking on the wood pellet grill and smoker. Try several things to discover a genuine crowd-pleaser.

2.5 Troubleshooting for The Most Common Problems

The Traeger grill might sometimes malfunction, like with other pellet grills. The grill splits as the temperature drops instead of igniting, and the pellets don't fall into the fire pit.

A troubleshooting guide may help you fix all the most typical issues.

You may call customer care or speak with your nearby Traeger dealer if you don't feel confident repairing yourself. Additionally, remember that the warranty is only for three years (in the United States). However, if you have some basic DIY abilities, most repairs are simple, and you can get any replacement parts on the Traeger website.

THE GRILL WON'T TURN ON.

Your Traeger grills may not be firing for one of three reasons. Your hot rod may not be heating up in the first place, your draft induction fan may not be operating, and your auger may not feed pellets into the fire pot in the third place.

The hot rod is fantastic because it is simple: it either works or doesn't. Removing the drip tray, the grill grate, and the heat baffle will allow you to determine this.

Place your hand on the fire pot at some distance to avoid hand burns and feel for heat while your grill is set on the smoke setting.

If you sense heat, you can tell whether your hot rod is operating correctly.

If your hot rod won't heat up, there's a good chance that one of the wires has been damaged.

If you see any friction in the wires or the connection that attaches to your controller, your hot rod must be replaced.

Calling 1-800 Traeger's customer care or visiting the website and placing an online purchase are the two best ways to replace it. Only the rod needs to be changed; the fire pot itself need not.

The draft induction fan not functioning is another frequent cause of your grill not starting up correctly.

Your fan is underneath your hopper; it's horizontal, making it extremely simple to see; and it will also have an orange wire coming off of it.

In certain cases, if you haven't used your grill in a while, oil, dirt, or sand buildup may be on it, preventing the fan from spinning.

Therefore, if you spin that fan when descending underneath your hopper, it will aid in getting it moving once more. A fan is necessary when using a wood pellet grill because it not only stokes the fire but also generates the convection that finally cooks your food.

Wires may cross below the fan when you put components within your grill, preventing the fan from spinning.

Grab a few zip ties, locate the few additional wires that are beneath the grill from your other components, zip them together, and remove them out of the way if your cables are obstructing the fan. You may let your fan whirl without restriction.

Check your drill since it isn't feeding pellets to the fire pot. It may also create problems.

The pellets are the fire's fuel; without them, your grill won't be able to generate any heat.

Wet pellets will be the most typical reason for an auger jam.

When exposed to moisture, the pellets quickly expand and get stuck within the auger shaft, making it impossible for the drill to spin pellets into the fire pot. Learn how to unclog an auger below.

The auger motor is situated in the hopper. A smaller fan is positioned vertically. If you see that it isn't spinning, you can either go to the website to buy a replacement or dial 1-800 Traeger to speak with a customer care representative.

2.6 Smoking, Grilling, Cooking and Baking on Your Traeger

BARBECUE

The actual definition of barbecue is as varied as the barbecues themselves. For our purposes, we will define barbecue as a method of cooking, either with direct or indirect heat, in which a hardwood-fired heat source is used. Barbecue is done at lower temperatures, usually below 400°F, separating it from grilling.

BAKE

Everything from pizza to brownies to apple pie can be cooked on your pellet grill. Giving that wood-fired smoky flavor to your baked goods might just be the flavor you have been missing.

The convection oven–style characteristics of a pellet grill make it perfect for baking. Because the air temperature is consistent throughout your chamber, baking can be done just as easily as in your kitchen oven.

Homemade wood-fired pizzas are always the go-to on the pellet grill, but you can do so much more, depending on your tastes and what local produce is in season. Wood-fired lasagna is a treat for any Italian food lover. Not sure what snack to grab for the kids? Fire up a pan of brownies!

BRAISE

Braising is a cooking method that uses both wet and dry cooking. Regarding a pellet grill, we braise primarily by cooking directly on the grill grate before placing the food into a liquid to complete its cooking. Multiple forms of dry cooking can be done before placing the item in liquid, including slow smoking. Wet cooking can open and close on your pellet grill or smoker. Shrimp, chili, and short ribs are wood-fired favorites for braising.

GRILL

Grilling is like barbecuing but at a higher temperature. When grilling, you cook meats quickly, never low and slow, but you'll still get that beautiful wood-fired flavor from your pellet grill. Grilling is for burgers, sausages, and more.

ROAST

Roasting is achieved by cooking your meat over high heat for a long period. It gives your meat an amazing crust while sealing in juices.

Roast your Christmas prime rib or leg of lamb in your pellet grill, and it'll be the hit of the party

THE MOST IMPORTANT INGREDIENT: TEMPERATURE

To be a pit master, you must learn to cook by temperature, not by time. Time is for baking; temperature is for meat.

The internal temperature of whatever you're cooking is the most important thing to look at when pulling anything from the grill—not color, shade, or anything else. Using temperature will prevent you from undercooking or overcooking your meats. The guide in the next subchapter shows you the proper internal temperature for meats discussed throughout this book.

THE STALL

The stall happens on longer cooks and typically occurs between 165°F and 170°F. The stall refers to a long period when your meat stays within a small temperature range.

To imagine the stall, think of your favorite football team. The game is tied; one second is left, and the opposing team is driving but fumbles on the one-yard line into the hands of a defensive tackle. That defensive lineman gets running, but at about the 70-yard line starts slowing down. Those next 30 yards take forever. That is the stall.

Even though you are going to get to the end of that cooking session and that All-Pro defensive tackle will make it to the end zone, you both have serious doubts. Just hunker down, grab another beer or two, and wait it out a couple of hours.

THE TEXAS CRUTCH

If that second beer just isn't an option, this is where the Texas crutch comes in. The Texas crutch is a method of wrapping meant to decrease the cooking time while maintaining moisture. By wrapping your brisket or pork shoulder with aluminum foil or butcher paper, you allow the meat to retain its moisture, even with consistent or increasing temperature.

To use the Texas crutch, wait until your meat has hit the stall (165°F) and wrap it with either foil or butcher paper for the remainder of the cook and rest time. If you can wait longer than 165°F, wait until 170°F. The longer you leave the meat exposed to smoke, the better the smoke flavor and the dryer the meat.

Going too high and too fast is not recommended; this is low-and-slow smoked barbecue.

There are arguments for wrapping and not wrapping, but if you ever have trouble with dry meat, use the Texas crutch; it's a simple way of preventing your meat from losing moisture, and if you are already using the crutch, use it earlier in the process.

SOMEONE LIKES IT SMOKED

Smoking isn't just for preserving anymore. Nowadays, smoking turkey and cheeses in supermarkets is common because people love the flavor. And, though brisket, ribs, and chicken are popular favorites, the good taste isn't limited to meats. Smoked vegetables, nuts, and even fruit are becoming mainstream delicacies.

Two methods are used with pellet grills: hot smoking and cold smoking. These two methods refer to the air temperature at the smoking time and give substantially different results.

There are many recipes best suited either for hot smoking or cold smoking. The recipes in this book touch on both methods and specify which type of smoking to use.

COLD SMOKING

Cold smoking is just what it sounds like: smoking at a lower temperature. Cold smoking on a pellet grill is typically done at temperatures between 80°F and 120°F in a chamber separate from the actual heat source. Cold smokes can be short or long, depending on your smoking.

Cold smoking is often used to preserve foods like smoked fish, jerky, and poultry. Cold smoking has been used for thousands of years worldwide to preserve meats for times when hunting and fishing were less of an option to provide food for a family.

Cold smoking can also be used as a method of adding flavor. Cheeses and nuts are primary examples of this. Cold smoking cheeses ~ like Cheddar and Havarti ~ and nuts ~ like almonds and cashews ~ will add that subtle smoke flavor we all enjoy without actually cooking the foods.

Most pellet grills do not come with a typical cold smoke option, but you can purchase them separately. Louisiana and Traeger Grills offer cold-smoker attachments.

HOT SMOKING

Hot smoking is done above 120°F and is the smoking functionality built into every pellet grill and smoker. Hot smoking is done in the same chamber as the smoke source or, in our case, the fire.

CLASSIC LOW-AND-SLOW SMOKING

Low-and-slow smoking is classic Southern, the most popular form of smoking in the United States and the rest of North America.

Low-and-slow smoking is done at temperatures between 180°F and 250°F, with the most common temperature being 225°F.

Low-and-slow smoking is what produces spectacular brisket and pulled pork. Just writing this has me imagining a plate full of sauced-up ribs, pulled pork, and brisket, with a heaping scoop of coleslaw on the side!

FINAL STEPS

One thing that surprises most entry-level grillers is that the post-cook time is as important as the pre-cook time. Resting, carving, and pulling can make or break your meats.

Have you ever had that perfect piece of meat—but when you cut into it, all the juices spilled out over the cutting board and out of the meat? Sure you have; we all have. This happens when the meat doesn't rest properly. It can be easily prevented, once again, with patience.

RESTING

As rest times vary from recipe to recipe, I'll include specific rest times in the recipes, but there's more to resting than just time.

If you aren't already using a Texas crutch, start wrapping your meat in foil or butcher paper when you pull it off the grill. After the initial wrapping, wrap it in old towels or blankets and place it in a cooler. This will keep your meat warm and allow it to continue to cook.

Always include rest time in your food preparation. Don't cut yourself short. By allowing your meat to rest, you continue to cook it and raise its internal temperature.

Also, let's not make rest time a bad thing. Use meats with long rest times for parties! Never let smoking or barbecuing be a limiting experience. Barbecue is about good times with good people and good food.

TENTING

Tenting is another form of letting your meat rest. In tenting, you use foil to create a tent above your meat. This process allows air to flow around the meat, preventing condensation and heat from rising and keeping your meat warm.

To create a tent, use a sheet of foil and fold it to build a triangular tent over your meat. (Ensure the foil is not directly touching the skin or meat.)

This is ideal for poultry and other meats with short rest times. Tent your Thanksgiving turkey while waiting for guests to arrive. If your steaks require rest time, tent them.

CARVING

Carving correctly ensures that your meat retains moisture and is easier to cut while eating.

When carving, be sure to have the right tools. A quality cutting board and a sharp knife are necessary. Other important tools include cutting gloves, a fork, and food serving gloves.

Sharpen your knives frequently at home or pay a professional to do it. Tough cuts and solid barks all need a sharp knife.

Also, like me, you like using your hands and not utensils. Grab your gloves. It gets hot, greasy, and just unsafe in there. Get your gloves on when you cut or pull any meat.

Chapter 3
Meat-Based Recipes

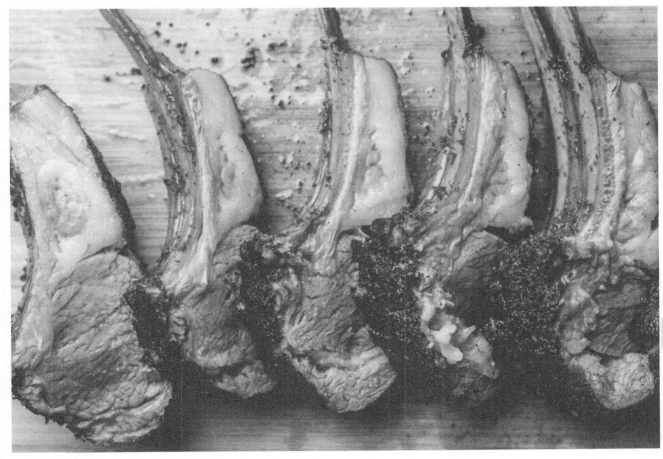

Maple and Bacon Chicken

Ingredients

◇ 1 teaspoon liquid smoke
◇ Salt as needed
◇ 4 skinless and boneless chicken breast
◇ Fresh pepper
◇ 12 uncooked slices of bacon
◇ ½ cup melted butter
◇ 1 cup maple syrup

PREPARATION:
20 MINUTES

COOKING TIME:
1 AND ½ HOURS

SERVINGS:
7

Directions:

1. Set your smoker's temperature to 250 degrees Fahrenheit.
2. Use salt and pepper to season the chicken.
3. Take three bacon slices and completely wrap the breast.
4. Use toothpicks to hold the bacon in place.
5. Mix butter, liquid smoke, and maple syrup in a medium bowl.
6. Keep one-third of this mixture aside for future use.
7. Place the chicken breast in the butter mixture and thoroughly coat it.
8. Put the chicken in the smoker, then place a pan within for about an hour to an hour and a half
9. The internal temperature of the chicken should reach 165 degrees Fahrenheit after 30 more minutes of smoking. Brush the chicken with the saved butter.
10. Enjoy!

Nutrition: Carbohydrates: 65 g Protein: 30 g: Cholesterol: 102 mg

Hellfire Chicken Wings

Ingredients:

- ◊ 2 tablespoons olive oil
- ◊ 3 pounds of chicken wings, tips removed

FOR THE SAUCE:

- ◊ 1/2 cup cilantro leaves
- ◊ 8 tablespoons unsalted butter
- ◊ 4 sliced crosswise jalapeno peppers
- ◊ 1/2 cup hot sauce

FOR THE RUB:

- ◊ 1 teaspoon salt
- ◊ 1 teaspoon onion powder
- ◊ 1 teaspoon garlic powder
- ◊ 1 teaspoon ground black pepper
- ◊ 1 tablespoon paprika
- ◊ 1 teaspoon celery seed
- ◊ 2 teaspoons brown sugar
- ◊ 1 teaspoon cayenne pepper

PREPARATION:
15 MINUTES

COOKING TIME:
40 MINUTES

SERVINGS:
6

Directions:

1. Start the Traeger grill by turning the knob, adding hickory-flavored wood pellets to the grill hopper, turning the grill on with the control panel, choosing "smoke" on the temperature dial, or setting the temperature to 350 degrees F and allowing it to heat for at least 15 minutes.
2. Prepare the chicken wings by removing the tips, slicing each wing through the joint into two portions, and placing them in a big dish.
3. Use a small bowl, add all ingredients, and whisk to blend while preparing the rub.
4. Then, toss the chicken wings until well covered after applying the prepared rub.

5. Meanwhile, when the grill is ready, open the lid, add the chicken wings to the grill grate, close the grill, and smoke for 40 minutes, flipping the wings halfway through until they are golden brown and the skin has become crisp.
6. Prepare the sauce in the meanwhile by melting the butter in a small skillet over low heat, adding the jalapeño, and cooking for 4 minutes.
7. After mixing in the spicy sauce and cilantro, remove the skillet from heat.
8. Transfer the finished chicken wings to a serving dish, cover with the prepared sauce, and stir to combine.

Nutrition: Carbohydrates: 51 g Protein: 46 g Cholesterol: 988 mg

Smoked, Candied, and Spicy Bacon

Ingredients:

◊ ½ cup brown sugar
◊ 1 lb. center-cut bacon
◊ ½ cup maple syrup
◊ ½ tablespoon pepper
◊ 1 tablespoon hot sauce

PREPARATION:
0 MINUTES

COOKING TIME:
40 MINUTES

SERVINGS:
10

Directions:

1. Mix the hot sauce, brown sugar, maple syrup, and pepper in a bowl.
2. Set your grill for wood pellets at 300 degrees.
3. The bacon pieces should be put on a lined baking sheet.
4. Evenly sprinkle the brown sugar mixture on both sides of the bacon pieces.
5. For 20 minutes, place the pan on your wood pellet grill. Turn the bacon slices over.
6. Once the bacon seems to be cooked and the sugar has dissolved, give them another 15 minutes.
7. After taking it off the grill, let it sit for 10 to 15 minutes.
8. Voila! Your candy bacon is prepared!

Nutrition: Carbohydrates: 37 g Protein: 9 g Cholesterol: 49 mg

Smoked Rack of Lamb

Ingredients:

◊ 1 rack of lamb rib, the membrane should be removed

FOR THE GLAZE:

◊ ¼ cup Dijon mustard
◊ 2 tablespoons soy sauce
◊ ¼ cup red wine
◊ 2 tablespoons Worcestershire sauce

FOR THE MARINADE:

◊ 2 teaspoons minced garlic
◊ 1 lemon, juiced
◊ 1 teaspoon dried basil
◊ 1 teaspoon salt
◊ 1 teaspoon dried thyme
◊ 1 teaspoon ground black pepper
◊ ¼ cup balsamic vinegar

PREPARATION:
10 MINUTES

COOKING TIME:
1H & 15 MINS

SERVINGS:
4

Directions:

1. Take a small bowl, add all the ingredients, and whisk to blend while you prepare the marinade.
2. In a large plastic bag, place the rack of lamb, pour the marinade in, close the bag, flip it upside down to coat the lamb with the marinade, and refrigerate for at least 8 hours.
3. When you're ready to start cooking, fire up the Traeger grill by turning it on with the control panel, loading the grill hopper with flavor-infused wood pellets, choosing "smoke" from the temperature dial, or setting the temperature to 300 degrees F and letting it heat up for at least five minutes.
4. Meanwhile, make the glaze by placing its components in a small bowl and whisking until incorporated.

5. Open the grill's lid after it has heated up, add the lamb rack to the grill grate, close it, and let it smoke for 15 minutes.
6. The lamb is brushed with glaze, turned over, and then smoked for 1 hour and 15 minutes, basting with glaze every 30 minutes, until the internal temperature has reached 145 degrees F.
7. When the lamb rack is finished cooking, move it to a cutting board, give it a 15-minute rest, slice it, and then serve.

Nutrition: Carbohydrates: 13 g Protein: 25 g Cholesterol: 98 mg

Smoked Chicken Drumsticks

Ingredients:

- ½ teaspoon thyme
- 2teaspoon garlic powder
- 10 chicken drumsticks
- 1teaspoon salt
- 1/2 teaspoon ground black pepper
- 1teaspoon onion powder
- ½ teaspoon cayenne pepper
- 1/3 cup hot sauce
- 1teaspoon brown sugar
- 1teaspoon paprika

PREPARATION:
10 MINUTES

COOKING TIME:
2H & 30 MINS

SERVINGS:
5

Directions:

1. Garlic powder, hot sauce, sugar, paprika, cayenne, thyme, salt, and ground pepper should all be combined in a large mixing basin. Toss the drumsticks in after adding them.
2. For one hour, cover the bowl in the refrigerator.
3. When the drumsticks are at room temperature, remove them from the marinade and let them rest for approximately an hour.
4. Prepare a rack for the drumsticks.
5. Start the fire in your pellet grill on smoke and leave the lid open for five minutes.
6. Use apple or hickory hardwood pellets to heat the grill to 250°F while keeping the lid closed.
7. Set the rack on your grill and smoke the drumsticks for 2 hours and 30 minutes until they are 180 degrees inside.
8. Drumsticks should be taken off the heat and given some time to set.
9. Serve.

Nutrition: Carbohydrates: 2.6 g Protein: 25.7 g Cholesterol: 81 mg

Chicken Fajitas on a Wood Pellet Grill

Ingredients:

◊ 1 tablespoon of Salt
◊ 1 large Red bell pepper
◊ 2 lbs. thinly sliced Chicken breast
◊ 1 large onion
◊ Seasoning mix
◊ 1 large orange bell pepper
◊ 2 tablespoons oil
◊ ½ tablespoon granulated garlic
◊ ½ tablespoon onion powder

PREPARATION:
0 MINUTES

COOKING TIME:
20 MINUTES

SERVINGS:
10

Directions:

1. Turn the grill on and preheat at 450 degrees.
2. Combine the oil and spices.
3. Add the slices of chicken.
4. Using a non-stick baking sheet, line a big pan.
5. For ten minutes, let the pan heat.
6. Grill the peppers, chicken, and other veggies.
7. Grill, the chicken for 10 minutes or until done.
8. Serve it hot off the grill with some warm tortillas and some vegetables.

Nutrition: Carbohydrates: 5 g Protein: 29 g Cholesterol: 77 mg

Garlic Parmesan Chicken Wings

Ingredients:

◊ 1 cup shredded parmesan cheese
◊ ½ cup chicken rub
◊ 5 pounds of chicken wings
◊ 3 tablespoons chopped parsley

FOR THE SAUCE:

◊ 1 cup unsalted butter
◊ 2 tablespoons chicken rub
◊ 5 teaspoons minced garlic

PREPARATION:
15 MINUTES

COOKING TIME:
20 MINUTES

SERVINGS:
6

Directions:

1. Start the Traeger grill by turning the knob, adding cherry-flavored wood pellets to the grill hopper, turning it on with the control panel, choosing "smoke" on the temperature dial, or setting the temperature to 450 degrees F and allowing it to heat for at least 15 minutes.
2. Meanwhile, throw the chicken wings in a big dish, add the chicken rub, and toss to cover the wings evenly.
3. Open the lid once the grill is ready, add the chicken wings to the grill grate, cover it, and smoke the food for 10 minutes on each side until the inside temperature reaches 165 degrees F.
4. Prepare the sauce in the meanwhile by placing all the ingredients in a medium saucepan over medium heat, cooking for 10 minutes, or until the sauce is smooth, and then putting the pan away until needed.
5. When finished, place chicken wings on a plate, cover with prepared sauce, stir to combine, top with cheese, garnish with parsley, and serve.

Nutrition: Carbohydrates: 8 g Protein: 0 g Cholesterol: 180 mg

Grilled Cuban Pork Chops

Ingredients:

◊ 1/3 cup extra virgin olive oil
◊ 4 thick-cut pork chops
◊ 1/2 orange, zest only
◊ 1 lime, zest
◊ 1 cup orange juice * freshly squeezed
◊ 1 cup finely chopped cilantro
◊ 4 cloves garlic, minced
◊ 1/4 cup chopped mint leaves
◊ 2- inch ginger, minced
◊ 2 teaspoons ground cumin
◊ 2 teaspoons dried oregano

PREPARATION:
6 HOURS

COOKING TIME:
7/8 MINUTES

SERVINGS:
4

Directions:

1. Lime juice, ginger, orange zest, olive oil, oregano, cilantro, cumin, and garlic should all be combined in a large mixing bowl.
2. 1/4 cup of this marinade should be set aside for future usage.
3. Add the pork chops to the marinade and let it marinate after being poured into a large mixing bowl.
4. Let set for six hours of marinating the pork chop.
5. Now place the grill grate inside and cover the grill.
6. Preheat for ten minutes at a high temperature.
7. Pork chops should be placed on the grill once preheated and cook for around 7 minutes at medium heat.
8. Open the appliance once the first half is through and turn the chops to cook the other side.
9. At the completion of cooking, the internal temperature should be 150 degrees Fahrenheit.
10. Serve once done.

Nutrition: Carbohydrates: 13.6 g Protein: 35.5 g Cholesterol: 80 mg

Homemade Meatballs

Ingredients:

◊ 2 slices of white bread
◊ 2 lbs. ground beef
◊ ½ cup whole milk
◊ ½ tablespoon onion powder
◊ 1 tablespoon salt
◊ 2 tablespoons Italian seasoning
◊ ½ tablespoon minced garlic
◊ ¼ tablespoon ground black pepper

PREPARATION:
0 MINUTES

COOKING TIME:
1 H & 20 M

SERVINGS:
12

Directions:

1. Black pepper, Italian seasoning, onion powder, chopped garlic, and white bread should all be combined.
2. Stir in the ground beef well.
3. Open the cover of your wood pellet grill for four to five minutes while preheating on the "smoke" setting.
4. Start by putting little balls on a lined baking sheet.
5. After 35 minutes of smoking, turn the balls.
6. Give it another 35 minutes to sit.
7. Serve it hot once it is golden brown.

Nutrition: Carbohydrates: 7 g Protein: 42 g Cholesterol: 137 mg

Stuffed Pork Crown Roast

Ingredients:

◊ 2 tablespoons apple cider vinegar
◊ 1 Snake River Pork Crown Roast or 12-14 ribs
◊ 1 cup apple juice
◊ 1 teaspoon salt
◊ 2 tablespoons Dijon mustard
◊ 1 tablespoon brown sugar
◊ 2 cloves of minced garlic
◊ 2 tablespoons freshly chopped rosemary or thyme
◊ ½ cup olive oil
◊ 8 cups of your favorite stuffing
◊ 1 teaspoon coarsely ground pepper

PREPARATION:
1 H & 20 M

COOKING TIME:
3 H & 30 M

SERVINGS:
2/4

Directions:

1. Place the meat on a level rack in a shallow roasting pan. Wrap a piece of foil around the bone's ends on both sides.

2. Boil the apple juice or cider for the marinade on high heat until it is reduced by about half. Whisk in the salt, thyme, brown sugar, pepper, vinegar, mustard, and vinegar after taking the mixture off the heat. After everything has been thoroughly combined, slowly whisk in the oil.

3. The marinade should be applied to the roast using a pastry brush. Make careful to evenly coat each surface. Plastic wrap should be used to enclose it completely. To get the beef to room temperature, let it rest for around 60 minutes.

4. Feel free to reapply the marinade to the roast at this point. Cover it and put it back in the refrigerator until it is ready to cook. Allow the meat to come to room temperature before cooking on the pellet grill. Before starting, ensure the grill has been warmed for around 15 minutes.

5. After grilling the meat for 30 minutes, turn down the grill's heat. The stuffing should be stuffed into the crown loosely and piled on top. With foil, properly enclose the filling. The stuffing may alternatively be baked in a skillet with the roast separately.

6. For a further 90 minutes, completely roast the meat. Remove the foil and continue roasting the stuffing for another 30 to 90 minutes, or until the pork reaches 150 degrees. Make careful not to contact the meat's bone with the temperature probe to avoid getting an inaccurate reading.

7. The roast should be taken off the grill. So that the meat can absorb all the juices, let it sit for about 15 minutes. The bones' foil wrapping should be removed. Leave the butcher's string attached until you're prepared to carve it. Transfer it to a heated dish at this point, slice it between the bones, and enjoy!

Nutrition: Carbohydrates: 5.5 g Protein: 107.9 g Cholesterol: 325.3 mg

Vegetable-Based Recipes

Chapter 4
Vegetable-Based Recipes

Roasted Parmesan Cheese Broccoli

Ingredients:

◊ 1 tablespoon lemon juice
◊ 3 cups broccoli, stems trimmed
◊ 1 tablespoon olive oil
◊ 1/2 teaspoon kosher salt
◊ 2 minced garlic cloves
◊ 1/2 teaspoon ground black pepper
◊ 1/8 cup grated parmesan cheese
◊ 1 teaspoon lemon zest

PREPARATION:
5 MINUTES

COOKING TIME:
45 MINUTES

SERVINGS:
3/4

Directions:

1. To 375°F, heat the pellet grill.
2. Put broccoli in a bag that can be sealed. Add pepper, salt, olive oil, lemon juice, and garlic cloves. Close the bag, then combine by throwing. Give the mixture 30 minutes to marinate.
3. Fill a grill basket with broccoli. To roast, place the basket on the grill grates. Broccoli should be grilled for 14 to 18 minutes, with a midway flip. Grill food till it's soft inside and slightly crispy on the exterior.
4. Broccoli should be taken off the grill, put on a serving platter, lemon zest added, and parmesan cheese sprinkled on top. Serve right away and delight in it!

Nutrition: Carbohydrates: 8.1 g Protein: 5.5 g Cholesterol: 1.8 mg

Grilled Cherry Tomato Skewers

Ingredients:

◊ 1 teaspoon kosher salt
◊ 1 tablespoon finely chopped fresh thyme
◊ 1/4 cup olive oil
◊ 24 cherry tomatoes
◊ 3 tablespoons balsamic vinegar
◊ 4 garlic cloves, minced
◊ 2 tablespoons finely chopped chives
◊ 1 teaspoon ground black pepper

PREPARATION:
10 MINUTES

COOKING TIME:
50 MINUTES

SERVINGS:
4

Directions:

1. Set the pellet grill to 425 °F.
2. In a medium bowl, combine olive oil, garlic, balsamic vinegar, and thyme. Add tomatoes, and toss to combine.
3. Allow tomatoes to marinate in the mixture for approximately 30 minutes at room temperature.
4. Thread four tomatoes per skewer after removing them from the marinade.
5. Use kosher salt and freshly ground pepper to season each side skewer.
6. Place on the grill grate and cook for 3 minutes until browned on both sides.
7. Remove off the grill and let food for a few minutes to rest. Add chives as a garnish before serving and enjoying!

Nutrition: Carbohydrates: 7 g Protein: 27 g Cholesterol: 70 mg

Smokey Roasted Cauliflower

Ingredients:

◊ 1 cup parmesan cheese
◊ 1 head cauliflower

SPICE INGREDIENTS:

◊ 1 teaspoon smoked paprika
◊ 2 cloves chopped garlic
◊ 1 tablespoon olive oil
◊ 1 teaspoon kosher salt

PREPARATION:
10 MINUTES

COOKING TIME:
1 H & 20 M

SERVINGS:
4/6

Directions:

1. To 180°F, preheat the pellet grill. Set the smoke setting to high if necessary.
2. Put the cauliflower on a grill basket after cutting it into bite-sized flowerets. Smoke the basket for an hour by placing it on the grill grate.
3. Combining the ingredients When the cauliflower is burning, in a small bowl. After an hour, take the cauliflower off the grill and let it cool.
4. Set the grill to 425 degrees Fahrenheit. Put the cauliflower in a sealable bag when it has cooled, then add the marinade. Put the mixture inside the bag.
5. Re-grill the cauliflower by placing it on a grill basket. Roast in the grill basket for 10 to 12 minutes or until the exteriors get crispy and golden.
6. Transfer to a serving plate after taking it from the grill. After covering the cauliflower with parmesan cheese, let it sit for a while so that it may melt. Distribute and savor!

Nutrition: Carbohydrates: 7 g Protein: 3 g Cholesterol: 0 mg

Crispy Maple Bacon Brussels Sprouts

Ingredients:

◊ 6 slices of thick-cut bacon
◊ 1/2 teaspoon ground black pepper
◊ 1 lb. trimmed and quartered brussels sprouts
◊ 3 tablespoon maple syrup
◊ 1/2 teaspoon kosher salt
◊ 1 teaspoon olive oil

PREPARATION:
15 MINUTES

COOKING TIME:
1 HOUR

SERVINGS:
6

Directions:

1. Set the pellet grill to 425 °F.
2. Make pieces of bacon that are 1/2 inch thick.
3. In the cast iron skillet, arrange the Brussels sprouts in a single layer. Add maple syrup and olive oil, then toss to coat. Add black pepper and kosher salt after scattering the bacon pieces on top.
4. Roast the Brussels sprouts in the pan over the pellet grill for 40 to 45 minutes, or until they are browned and caramelized.
5. After taking the pan from the grill, let the brussels sprouts cool for five to ten minutes. Distribute and savor!

Nutrition: Carbohydrates: 13.6 g Protein: 4.8 g Cholesterol: 6.6 mg

Grilled Broccoli

Ingredients:

◊ 1 teaspoon of lemon pepper
◊ 1 tablespoon of canola oil
◊ 2 cups of broccoli, fresh

Directions:

1. Close the hood after inserting the grill and grate.
2. Turn the grill on high for ten minutes to preheat it.
3. Combine lemon pepper, broccoli, and canola oil in the meanwhile.
4. Toss ingredients well to coat them.
5. Once more food appears, place it on a grill grate.
6. Cook at medium heat for 3 minutes with the unit locked.
7. Serve after taking out.

Nutrition: Carbohydrates: 6.7 g Protein: 2.7 g Cholesterol: 0 mg

PREPARATION:
15 MINUTES

COOKING TIME:
3 MINUTES

SERVINGS:
1/2

Smoked Tomato and Mozzarella Dip

Ingredients:

◊ ½ teaspoon onion powder
◊ 1 teaspoon dried basil
◊ 8 ounces shredded Colby cheese
◊ 8 ounces shredded smoked mozzarella cheese
◊ 1 cup sour cream
◊ ½ cup grated parmesan cheese
◊ 1 cup sun-dried tomatoes
◊ 1 teaspoon fresh ground pepper
◊ 1 and ½ teaspoon salt
◊ 1 teaspoon dried oregano
◊ French toast, serving
◊ 1 teaspoon red pepper flakes
◊ 1 minced garlic clove

PREPARATION:
5 MINUTES

COOKING TIME:
1 HOUR

SERVINGS:
4

Directions:

1. Using your favorite wood, heat the smoker to 275 degrees Fahrenheit.
2. The tomatoes, cheeses, pepper, basil, salt, oregano, garlic, red pepper flakes, and onion powder should all be combined in a big bowl.
3. Put the mixture in a small metal pan and place it on a smoker.
4. Smoke for one hour.
5. Serve with some toasted French bread
6. Enjoy your meal.

Nutrition: Carbohydrates: 15 g Protein: 46 g Cholesterol: 11 mg

Green Beans with Bacon

Ingredients:

◊ 1.1/2 pound green beans, ends trimmed
◊ 4 chopped strips of bacon
◊ 1teaspoon minced garlic
◊ 4tablespoons olive oil
◊ 1teaspoon salt

PREPARATION:
10 MINUTES

COOKING TIME:
20 MINUTES

SERVINGS:
6

Directions:

1. Start the Traeger grill by turning the knob, adding flavorful wood pellets to the grill hopper, turning the grill on the control panel, choosing "smoke" on the temperature dial, or setting the temperature to 450 degrees F and letting it heat up for at least 15 minutes.
2. In the meantime, take a sheet tray, combine all ingredients, and stir.
3. Open the grill's lid after it has heated up, set the prepared sheet tray on the grill grate, close it, and smoke the food for 20 minutes or until it is slightly browned and cooked.
4. Transfer the finished green beans to a serving dish before serving.

Nutrition: Carbohydrates: 8.2 g Protein: 5.9 g Cholesterol: 4.6 mg

Vegetable Sandwich

Ingredients:

FOR THE SMOKED HUMMUS:

◊ 1 tablespoon minced garlic
◊ 1/3 cup tahini
◊ 1.1/2 cups cooked chickpeas
◊ 1 teaspoon salt
◊ 2 tablespoons olive oil
◊ 1 tablespoon lemon juice

FOR THE CHEESE:

◊ ½ teaspoon minced garlic
◊ 1 lemon, juiced
◊ ¼ teaspoon salt
◊ ¼ teaspoon ground black pepper
◊ 1/2 cup ricotta cheese

FOR THE VEGETABLES:

◊ 1 small eggplant, sliced into strips, destemmed
◊ 2 large portobello mushrooms
◊ 1 teaspoon salt
◊ ½ teaspoon ground black pepper
◊ 1 trimmed small zucchini, sliced into strips
◊ ¼ cup olive oil
◊ 1 peeled small yellow squash, sliced into strips

PREPARATION:
30 MINUTES

COOKING TIME:
45 MINUTES

SERVINGS:
4

TO ASSEMBLE:

◊ 2 heirloom tomatoes, sliced
◊ 1 bunch basil, leaves chopped
◊ 4 ciabatta buns, halved

Directions:

1. Start the Traeger grill by turning the knob, adding pecan-flavored wood pellets to the grill hopper, turning it on with the control panel, choosing "smoke" on the temperature dial, or setting the temperature to 180 degrees F and allowing it to heat for at least 15 minutes.
2. Prepare the hummus in the meantime by spreading chickpeas on a sheet tray.
3. Open the lid once the grill is ready, lay a sheet tray on the grill grate, close the grill, and smoke the food for 20 minutes.
4. Transfer the cooked chickpeas to a food processor along with the additional ingredients, and process until smooth, about 2 minutes. Set aside until needed.
5. Adjust the smoking heat temperature to 500 degrees Fahrenheit, secure the cover, and wait 10 minutes for it to warm.
6. Veggies should be prepared in the meanwhile. To do this, take a big bowl, add all the vegetables, season with salt and pepper, drizzle with lemon juice and oil and toss to combine.
7. Vegetables should be placed on the grill grate, covered, and smoked for 15 minutes for mushrooms and 25 minutes for zucchini, eggplant, and squash.
8. Meanwhile, make the cheese by placing its components in a small bowl and stirring until everything is well blended.
9. Cut the buns in half lengthwise, put the prepared hummus on one side, and sprinkle the cheese on the other. Stuff the sandwich with the grilled veggies, and then top it with the basil and tomatoes.
10. Serve immediately.

Nutrition: Carbohydrates: 45 g Protein: 8.3 g mg Cholesterol: 40 mg

Cauliflower with Parmesan and Butter

Ingredients:

◊ 1 teaspoon minced garlic
◊ One medium head of cauliflower
◊ 1teaspoon salt
◊ 1/4 cup olive oil
◊ ½ teaspoon ground black pepper
◊ 1/2 cup unsalted melted butter
◊ 1/4 cup shredded parmesan cheese
◊ 1/2 tablespoon chopped parsley

PREPARATION:
15 MINUTES

COOKING TIME:
45 MINUTES

SERVINGS:
4

Directions:

1. Start the Traeger grill by turning the knob, adding flavorful wood pellets to the grill hopper, turning the grill on the control panel, choosing "smoke" on the temperature dial, or setting the temperature to 450 degrees F and letting it heat up for at least 15 minutes.
2. The cauliflower head should be brushed with oil, salted and peppered, and then placed in a frying pan.
3. Open the grill lid after it has heated up, set the prepared skillet pan on the grill grate, close the grill, and smoke for 45 minutes, or until the middle is soft and golden brown.
4. Meanwhile, melt the butter in a small bowl and toss the parsley, cheese, and garlic until incorporated.
5. When the final 20 minutes of cooking are up, baste the cheese mixture periodically. When finished, turn off the heat and top the cauliflower with parsley.
6. After cutting it into pieces, serve.

Nutrition: Carbohydrates: 10.8 g Protein: 7.4 g Cholesterol: 7.6 mg

Feisty Roasted Cauliflower

Ingredients:

◊ 1 tablespoon oil
◊ 1 cauliflower head, cut into florets
◊ 1 cup grated parmesan
◊ ¼ teaspoon paprika
◊ ½ teaspoon pepper
◊ 2 crushed garlic cloves
◊ ½ teaspoon salt

PREPARATION:
15 MINUTES

COOKING TIME:
10 MINUTES

SERVINGS:
4

Directions:

1. Set your smoker to 180 degrees Fahrenheit.
2. Place florets in the smoker, then smoke for one hour.
3. Place all ingredients in a bowl except the cheese.
4. Remove the florets after smoking
5. Turn the heat to 450 degrees Fahrenheit, brush the florets with the brush, and place them on the grill.
6. Smoke for another ten minutes.
7. Spread cheese on top and leave it there till it melts (lid closed).
8. Distribute and savor!

Nutrition: Carbohydrates: 7 g Protein: 47 g Cholesterol: 45 mg

Smoked Vegetables

Ingredients

◊ 2 zucchini sliced
◊ 1 package of mushrooms halved
◊ 1/2 onion diced
◊ 2 yellow squash sliced
◊ 1.5 teaspoons garlic salt
◊ pepper to taste
◊ 3 tablespoons butter sliced
◊ 2 tablespoons olive oil

PREPARATION:
10 MINUTES

COOKING TIME:
20 MINUTES

SERVINGS:
6

Directions:

1. Fire up the grill to 400 degrees. Round up the zucchini, squash, and mushrooms. Cut the onion into cubes. Place in a basin.
2. Olive oil and spices should be added. Mix in the vegetables.
3. Put the mixture into an aluminum 9x13" pan and top with butter slices. Wrap with foil.
4. Open the smoker when it hits 400 degrees, place the tray inside, then reduce the heat to 350 degrees.
5. 20 to 25 minutes of cooking (total time for it to get ready would depend on how tender you like them)

Nutrition: Carbohydrates: 6 g Protein: 3 g Cholesterol: 15 mg

Chapter 5
Fish-Based Recipes

Blackened Catfish

Ingredients:

◊ 1 teaspoon granulated garlic
◊ Spice blend
◊ 1/4 teaspoon cayenne pepper
◊ 1 teaspoon ground thyme
◊ 1/2 cup Cajun seasoning
◊ 1 teaspoon ground oregano
◊ 1 tablespoon smoked paprika
◊ 1/2 cup butter
◊ 1 teaspoon onion powder
◊ 1 teaspoon pepper
◊ 4 catfish fillets
◊ Fish
◊ Salt to taste

PREPARATION:
0 MINUTES

COOKING TIME:
40 MINUTES

SERVINGS:
4

Directions:

1. All the spice blend components should be combined in a bowl.
2. Apply the salt and spice mixture to the fish's two sides.
3. Your wood pellet grill should be at 450 degrees Fahrenheit.
4. The butter is added after heating the cast iron pan. To the pan, add the fillets.
5. Cook each side for 5 minutes.
6. Lemon wedges may be used as a garnish while serving.
7. Before seasoning, smoke the catfish for 20 minutes.

Nutrition: Carbohydrates: 2.9 g Protein: 19.2 g Cholesterol: 65.8 mg

Mussels with Pancetta Aioli

Ingredients:

◊ 1 tablespoon minced garlic, or more to taste
◊ ¾ cup mayonnaise
◊ 1.4-ounce chopped slice pancetta
◊ 4 pounds of mussels
◊ ¼ cup good-quality olive oil
◊ Salt and pepper
◊ 8 thick slices of Italian bread

PREPARATION:
15 MINUTES

COOKING TIME:
30 MINUTES

SERVINGS:
4

Directions:

1. In a small bowl, combine the garlic and mayonnaise using a whisk. In a small, chilly skillet, add the pancetta. Reduce the heat to low and cook, stirring periodically, for approximately 5 minutes, or until most of the fat has rendered and the pork is brown and crisp. Drain on a paper towel, then add 1 teaspoon of the rendered pan fat to the mayonnaise. If desired, taste and add additional salt and garlic. Until you are ready to serve, cover and chill the dish. (The aoli may be prepared several days in advance; store in the refrigerator in an airtight container.)

2. For direct heat cooking, light the coals or preheat a gas grill. Verify the cleanliness of the grates.

3. Remove any beards and rinse the mussels. Any that breaks or doesn't close when tapped should be thrown away.

4. Brush the bread slices with oil on both sides. Place the bread directly over the flames on the grill. Close the cover and toast each side for 1 to 2 minutes, rotating once, until grill marks and some charring appear. Take off the grill, then keep warm.

5. Spread out the mussels, so they are in a single layer and scatter them onto the grill directly over the flame. Put the cover on right away and cook for 3 minutes. Using tongs, move the

open mussels into a big dish. Close the top and cook for another minute or two if none have opened. Suppose any have, remove the open mussels from the grill and continue doing so until all are done.

6. With a big spoon, spread the aioli over the mussels' tops and flip them over to coat them. Serve the bread on top of (or next to) the mussels, drizzled with their juices.

Nutrition: Carbohydrates: 14.95 g Protein: 9.57 g Cholesterol: 0 mg

Cajun Seasoned Shrimp

Ingredients:

◊ 1/2 teaspoon of Cajun seasoning
◊ 20 pieces of jumbo Shrimp
◊ 1 teaspoon of magic shrimp seasoning
◊ 1 tablespoon of Canola oil

PREPARATION:
10 MINUTES

COOKING TIME:
20 MINUTES

SERVINGS:
4

Directions:

1. Shrimp, canola oil, and spices should all be placed in a large bowl.
2. Mix well for a fine coating.
3. Put the shrimp on skewers right away.
4. Place the grill grate into the grill and warm it for 8 minutes on high.
5. Open the grill after it has been prepared, then insert the shrimp skewers.
6. For two minutes, cook the shrimp.
7. Flip the shrimp, open the unit, and cook them for an additional two minutes at medium.
8. When done, serve.

Nutrition: Carbohydrates: 23.9 g Protein: 50.2 g Cholesterol: 350 mg

Peppercorn Tuna Steaks

Ingredients:

◊ 2 pounds of yellowfin tuna
◊ ¼ cup of salt
◊ ¼ cup Dijon mustard
◊ 2 tablespoons peppercorn
◊ Freshly ground black pepper

Directions:

1. Take a big container and combine salt and warm water in it (enough water to cover the fish)
2. Place the tuna on the cover for eight hours, brine, and chill.
3. Prepare your smoker with your favorite wood at 250 degrees Fahrenheit.
4. Take out the tuna and wipe it dry.
5. Transfer to the grill pan, then cover with Dijon mustard.
6. Add pepper and peppercorn for seasoning.
7. Place the tuna in the smoker and cook for one hour.
8. Enjoy!

Nutrition: Carbohydrates: 28 g Protein: 52 g Cholesterol: 250 mg

PREPARATION: 8 HOURS

COOKING TIME: 10 MINUTES

SERVINGS: 3

Togarashi Smoked Salmon

Ingredients:

◊ Togarashi for seasoning
◊ Salmon filet - 2 large

FOR BRINE:

◊ Water - 4 cups
◊ Brown sugar - 1 cup
◊ Kosher salt - ⅓ cup

PREPARATION:
16 HOURS

COOKING TIME:
20H & 15M

SERVINGS:
10

Directions:

1. The fish filet has to be free of any thorns.
2. Blend each brine component well until the brown sugar has entirely dissolved.
3. Place the filet in a large bowl with the mixture.
4. For 16 hours, place the bowl in the refrigerator.
5. Remove the fish from this mixture after 16 hours. Then, dry it off.
6. Put the salmon in the fridge for a further 2-4 hours. (This action is crucial. DON'T MISS IT.)
7. Apply togarashi to your salmon filet to season.
8. Place the fish on the wood pellet grill and turn on the "smoke" setting.
9. Smoke for four hours.
10. Ensure the temperature doesn't fall below 130 degrees or rise over 180.
11. Take it off the grill, reheat it up and serve it with a side dish of your choice.

Nutrition: Carbohydrates: 19 g Protein: 10 g Cholesterol: 29 mg

Traeger Grilled Rockfish Recipe

Ingredients:

◊ 1 lemon, sliced
◊ 6 rockfish filets
◊ 3/4 teaspoon Himalayan salt
◊ 1/2 teaspoon garlic powder
◊ 6 tablespoons of butter
◊ 2 teaspoons chopped fresh dill
◊ 1/2 teaspoon onion powder

PREPARATION:
10 MINUTES

COOKING TIME:
20 MINUTES

SERVINGS:
6

Directions:

1. Following the manufacturer's recommendations, preheat your Traeger grill to 375°.
2. Put the fish in a baking dish that can be used on a grill. Put the fish inside and sprinkle both sides with salt, garlic, onion, and dill powder.
3. Add a slice of lemon and a pat of butter to the top of each filet.
4. Close the grill's cover after placing the baking pan on it. Cook the fish for 20 minutes until it is flaky and translucent.
5. After removing from the grill, wait five minutes before serving.

Nutrition: Carbohydrates: 2 g Protein: 28 g Cholesterol: 98 mg

Traeger Blackened Fish Tacos

Ingredients:

◊ 4 tablespoons blackening seasoning
◊ 18 ounces of fresh fish filets
◊ Limes for garnish
◊ Corn tortillas
◊ Shredded cabbage

PREPARATION:
5 MINUTES

COOKING TIME:
10 MINUTES

Directions:

1. According to manufacturer recommendations, preheat your Traeger grill at 400 degrees. While it is heated, put your cast iron pan within.
2. Give your fish a generous coating of blackening seasoning.
3. Carefully take the pan from the grill using a pot holder and thoroughly spray it with cooking spray. (Avoid misting it while it's grilling! The cooking spray may catch fire!)
4. Place the fish into the pan as soon as it is back on the grill, then cover it with the lid.
5. Grill for 4-5 minutes until a crust has formed and the bottom is browned.
6. Make one careful flip of the fish using a large spatula. Cook for a further 4-5 minutes with the lid on.
7. Depending on how thick your filets are, you must cook fish for a certain time. Compared to thick filets, thinner filets will cook more rapidly.
8. Your fish is cooked; the flaky flesh within is no longer transparent.
9. Serve with your favorite taco fixings, corn tortillas, and limes!

SERVINGS:
6

Nutrition: Carbohydrates:3 g Protein: 21 g Cholesterol: 80 mg

Teriyaki Smoked Shrimp

Ingredients:

◊ ½ tablespoon onion powder
◊ 1 lb. uncooked shrimp
◊ ½ tablespoon salt
◊ ½ tablespoon garlic powder
◊ 4 tablespoon mayo
◊ 4 tablespoon teriyaki sauce
◊ 2 tablespoons minced green onion

PREPARATION:
0 MINUTES

COOKING TIME:
20 MINUTES

SERVINGS:
6

Directions:

1. Wash the shrimp well after removing the shells.
2. 450 degrees should be the grill's temperature.
3. Use salt, garlic powder and onion powder for seasoning.
4. Cook the shrimp for a total of 5 to 6 minutes.
5. After being cooked, take the shrimp off the grill and top it with mayo, spring onions, and teriyaki sauce.

Nutrition: Carbohydrates: 2 g Protein: 16 g Cholesterol: 190 mg

Lobster Tails

Ingredients:

◊ 2lobster tails, 10 ounces each

FOR THE SAUCE:

◊ 1/4 teaspoon garlic salt
◊ 2 tablespoons chopped parsley
◊ 1teaspoon paprika
◊ 2 tablespoons lemon juice
◊ 1/4 teaspoon old bay seasoning
◊ 1/4 teaspoon ground black pepper
◊ 8 tablespoons butter, unsalted

PREPARATION:
10 MINUTES

COOKING TIME:
35 MINUTES

SERVINGS:
4

Directions:

1. Start the Traeger grill by turning the knob, adding flavorful wood pellets to the grill hopper, turning the grill on the control panel, choosing "smoke" on the temperature dial, or setting the temperature to 450 degrees F and letting it heat up for at least 15 minutes.
2. Prepare the sauce by taking a small saucepan, setting it over medium-low heat, adding the butter, and adding the other ingredients when it melts. Stir until incorporated and leave away until needed.
3. Use kitchen shears to cut the lobster's shell from the center to the tail. After that, remove the flesh from the shell while leaving the meat connected at the base of the crab's tail.
4. Then, cut the crab flesh in half to create butterfly-shaped pieces, arrange the lobster tails on a baking sheet, cover each with 1 tablespoon of the sauce, and set aside the remaining sauce.
5. Open the top once the grill is ready, add the crab tails to the grill grate, close the lid, and smoke the crabs for 30 minutes until they are opaque.
6. When finished, place the lobster tails on a plate and top with the leftover sauce.

Nutrition: Carbohydrates: 1 g Protein: 20 g Cholesterol: 22 mg

Halibut in Parchment

Ingredients:

◊ 2 ears of corn kernels
◊ 16 trimmed asparagus spears, sliced into 1/2-inch pieces
◊ 4 ounces of halibut fillets, remove the pin bones
◊ Salt as needed
◊ 2 lemons, cut into 12 slices
◊ Ground black pepper as required
◊ 2 tablespoons chopped parsley
◊ 2 tablespoons olive oil

PREPARATION:
15 MINUTES

COOKING TIME:
15 MINUTES

SERVINGS:
4

Directions:

1. Start the Traeger grill by turning the knob, adding flavorful wood pellets to the grill hopper, turning the grill on the control panel, choosing "smoke" on the temperature dial, or setting the temperature to 450 degrees F and letting it heat for at least five minutes.
2. Cut out parchment paper that is 18 inches long, set a fillet in the middle of each piece, season with salt and pepper, and then sprinkle oil over it.
3. Sprinkle one-fourth of the asparagus and corn on each fillet, cover with three lemon slices that are slightly overlapped, season with salt and black pepper, and then close the fillets and veggies snugly to prevent the steam from leaking the packet.
4. Open the grill's lid after it has heated up, lay the fillet packets on the grill grate, close it, and smoke for 15 minutes, or until the packets have begun to turn a light brown puff up.
5. When finished, move the packets to a plate, let them stand for 5 minutes, then gently open each one by cutting an 'X' in the middle, revealing the fillets and veggies. Finally, top with parsley and serve.

Nutrition: Carbohydrates: 14.2 g Protein: 25.7 g Cholesterol: 186 mg

Chapter 6
Soups and
Snacks Recipes

Chicken Tortilla Soup

Ingredients:

◊ 1 Jalapeno Pepper, seeds removed and halved
◊ 1/2 cup canned Black Beans
◊ 1-1/2 cup Chicken Stock
◊ 1/2 peeled and halved Onion
◊ 2 Carrots, sliced into ¼-inch pieces
◊ 1/2 cup of Corn
◊ 14-1/2 oz. Fire Roasted Tomatoes
◊ 3 Garlic cloves
◊ 10 oz. Chicken Breast, diced into ½ inch
◊ 1/4 cup Cilantro Leaves

PREPARATION:
10 MINUTES

COOKING TIME:
35 MINUTES

SERVINGS:
4

FOR THE SEASONING MIX:

◊ 1 teaspoon. Cumin
◊ 1/4 teaspoon. Chipotle
◊ 1/2 teaspoon. Smoked Paprika
◊ 1/2 teaspoon. Sea Salt

Directions:

1. Put the onion, cilantro, carrots, pepper, and garlic cloves in the blender's pitcher.
2. After three minutes of pulsing, add the chicken stock to the mixture.
3. For an additional three minutes, pulse.
4. Then combine all of the ingredients and press "hearty soup."
5. Transfer, lastly, to the serving dish.

Nutrition: Carbohydrates: 40 g Protein: 14 g Cholesterol: 20 mg

Minestrone Soup

Ingredients:

◊ 2 tablespoons. Olive Oil
◊ 1/4 teaspoon. Black Pepper
◊ 15 oz. Cannellini Beans
◊ 1/2 teaspoon. Salt
◊ 1 Onion quartered
◊ 2 minced Garlic cloves
◊ 2 minced Rosemary sprigs
◊ 1/3 cup grated Parmesan Cheese
◊ 1 cup Kale leaves, chopped
◊ Juice and Zest of 1 Lemon
◊ 4cups Vegetable Stock

PREPARATION:
10 MINUTES

COOKING TIME:
35 MINUTES

SERVINGS:
4

Directions:

1. Keep the onion, oil, and garlic in the blender's pitcher to start.
2. Select the saute button next.
3. Stir and add celery, vegetable stock, rosemary, lemon zest, kale, lemon juice, salt, parmesan, and pepper once the ingredients have been sautéed.
4. Then choose "hearty soup" from the menu.
5. Add the beans and continue cooking until just 5 to 6 minutes remain.

Nutrition: Carbohydrates: 4.7 g Protein: 1.8 g Cholesterol: 1 mg

Spinach Soup

Ingredients:

◊ 2 tablespoons. Vegetable Oil
◊ 2 cups Chicken Stock
◊ 1 Onion quartered
◊ ½ lb. thinly sliced Red Potatoes,
◊ 2 ½ cup Spinach
◊ 2 cups Milk, whole
◊ 1 Bay Leaf
◊ Black Pepper and Sea Salt, as needed
◊ 1 Leek, large and sliced thinly
◊ 1 Thyme Sprigs

PREPARATION:
10 MINUTES

COOKING TIME:
35 MINUTES

SERVINGS:
4

Directions:

1. Put the oil, bay leaf, onion, and thyme in the blender pitcher to make this nutritious soup.
2. Press the "saute" button now.
3. After the ingredients have been sautéed, whisk in the other ingredients and choose "smooth soup."
4. Last but not least, ladle the hot soup into the serving dishes.

Nutrition: Carbohydrates: 32 g Protein: 15 g Cholesterol: 66 mg

Ramen Soup

Ingredients:

◊ 1 cup Chicken, cooked and cut into 1-inch cubes
◊ 1 tablespoon. Extra Virgin Olive Oil
◊ 4 cups Chicken Stock
◊ 2 Baby Bok Choy Head, leaves torn
◊ 3 oz. dried Ramen
◊ 1 Shallot, chopped into a 1-inch piece
◊ 4 Garlic cloves
◊ 2 teaspoons. fresh Ginger
◊ 1 teaspoon. toasted Sesame Oil
◊ One bunch of thinly sliced Green Onion

PREPARATION:
10 MINUTES

COOKING TIME:
35 MINUTES

SERVINGS:
2

Directions:

1. Keep the garlic, shallot, ginger, and olive oil in the blender pitcher first.
2. Press the "saute" button after that.
3. After that, include the chicken, chicken stock, green onions, and sesame oil.
4. Select the "hearty soup" option at this point.
5. Put the baby bok choy and ramen noodles in three minutes before the show stops.
6. If the chicken is cooked to an internal temperature of 165°F, transfer the soup to the serving dishes.
7. Serve right away.

Nutrition: Carbohydrates: 25 g Protein: 3 g Cholesterol: 2.5 mg

Ancho-Dusted Jícama Sticks with Lime

Ingredients:

◊ 2 tablespoons good-quality olive oil
◊ 1/2-pound trimmed and peeled jícama
◊ 2 teaspoons ancho chile powder
◊ 1 lime, cut into wedges
◊ Salt

PREPARATION:
15 MINUTES

COOKING TIME:
30 MINUTES

Directions:

1. For medium-high direct cooking, light the coals or preheat the gas grill. Verify the cleanliness of the grates.

2. Slice the jicama into a 1 1/2-inch piece. Olive oil should be brushed on both sides of the slices. Slices should be placed immediately over the flames on the grill. Close the cover and cook on each side for 7 to 10 minutes, flipping once until grill marks appear.

3. Slice the jicama into 1-inch-wide sticks, then transfer the sticks to a chopping board. Place on a serving plate, sprinkle with salt to taste, and ancho powder, tossing to coat well. Serve after squeezing the lime wedges over them and flipping them one more to coat evenly.

SERVINGS:
8

Nutrition: Carbohydrates: 12 g Protein: 1 g Cholesterol: 0 mg

Pizza Bianca

Ingredients:

◊ 2 teaspoons instant yeast
◊ 3 cups all-purpose or bread flour, and more as required
◊ 2 teaspoons coarse sea or kosher salt, and some more for sprinkling
◊ 1 tablespoon or more chopped fresh rosemary
◊ 2 tablespoons good-quality olive oil, and some more for drizzling

PREPARATION:
30 MINUTES

COOKING TIME:
3 HOURS

SERVINGS:
2

Directions:

1. In a large basin, combine the yeast, salt, and flour. Mix with a large spoon after adding the oil and 1 cup of water. One tablespoon of water at a time, keep adding it until the dough comes together into a ball and feels somewhat sticky to the touch. In the odd case that the mixture becomes too sticky, add flour by the spoonful until the proper consistency is reached.

2. Spread some light flour on a work area and spread the dough there. Form into a ball by giving it a smooth minute of hand kneading. Place the dough in a basin, wrap it in plastic wrap, and place it somewhere warm to rise for one to two hours, or until it has doubled in size. If you're in a rush, you may shorten this rising period; alternatively, you can let the dough rise gradually in the refrigerator for up to 8 hours. The dough may now be frozen for up to a month: Put it in a zipper bag or carefully wrap it in plastic. Frozen items should be brought to room temperature before being shaped.

3. Divide the dough into two or more pieces, and then form each piece into a ball. Each ball should be placed on a work surface that has been gently dusted with flour, floured, and covered with plastic wrap or a towel. Allow resting for 25 to 30 minutes, or until somewhat puffy.

4. For medium-direct cooking, start the coals or fire up the gas grill. Verify the cleanliness of the grates.

5. Each ball should be rolled or gently pressed into a flat, circular disk. If required, carefully

dust the work surface and the dough to prevent sticking (use only as much flour as you need). Push down in the middle and outward to the edge, twisting the round as you go to expand the dough. If you're creating two pizzas, aim for circles 10 to 12 inches in diameter and keep pressing down, spreading out, and flipping the dough until it is the size you need. Olive oil should be drizzled over the tops after the rosemary, and a little coarse salt has been distributed uniformly.

6. Over the flames, place the crusts on the grill. Depending on the fire's height, cook for 5 to 10 minutes with the lid on, or until the bottoms are firm and browned and the tops are well cooked. The top side of the dough will bubble up from the heat beneath but probably won't color much. Slice into wedges or tiny pieces with a pizza cutter on a cutting board before serving.

Nutrition: Carbohydrates: 56 g Protein: 18 g Cholesterol: 20 mg

Grilled Plantains

Ingredients:

◊ 1 tablespoon melted coconut oil
◊ 2 Plantains, cut and sliced horizontally

Directions:

1. Place the grill grate into the grill and warm it for 8 minutes on high.
2. Open the appliance after the grill has warmed up.
3. Add the plantains to the hot grill after brushing them with coconut oil.
4. Cook for 3 minutes at medium heat with the device closed.
5. Cook for three more minutes after flipping to cook from the other side.
6. Serve once finished.

Nutrition: Carbohydrates: 57.1 g Protein: 2.3 g Cholesterol: 0 mg

PREPARATION:
0 MINUTES

COOKING TIME:
6 MINUTES

SERVINGS:
2

Grilled Watermelon

Ingredients:

◊ 2 tablespoons honey
◊ 6 watermelon slices, 1-inch thick and 3 inches each cross

Directions:

1. Close the unit after putting the grill grate within the hood.
2. Set the timer for two minutes and the temperature to the maximum. As the unit gets heated up, stop it.
3. Apply honey to the watermelon slices at this time.
4. Spray some oil onto the barbecue grates.
5. Put the slices of watermelon on the grill grate.
6. For two minutes, with the hood closed, cook the food without turning it.
7. Slices of the watermelon should be served right away after being finished.

Nutrition: Carbohydrates: 81.8 g Protein: 5.1 g Cholesterol: 0 mg

PREPARATION:
5 MINUTES

COOKING TIME:
2 MINUTES

SERVINGS:
2/3

Rosemary Cheese Bread

Ingredients:

◊ ½ teaspoon sea salt
◊ 1½ cup sunflower seeds
◊ 1 egg
◊ 2 teaspoon xanthan gum
◊ 2 cups grated mozzarella
◊ 1 teaspoon finely chopped fresh rosemary
◊ 2 tablespoons cream cheese

PREPARATION:
10 MINUTES

COOKING TIME:
12 MINUTES

SERVINGS:
30
BREADSTICK

Directions:

1. With the lid covered, preheat the grill to 400°F for 15 minutes.
2. Put the sunflower seeds in a strong blender and process until the mixture resembles flour.
3. Add the rosemary, xanthan gum, and sunflower seed flour to a mixing bowl. Combine, then reserve.
4. In the microwave, melt the cheese. In order to achieve this, put the mozzarella cheese and cream cheese on a plate that can be heated in the microwave.
5. Heat the cheese for one minute on high in the microwave-safe container.
6. Take the dish out, then stir it. Cook the meal for 30 seconds on the grill. The dish should be brought out and smoothed out.
7. Into a large mixing bowl, pour the melted cheese.
8. When the cheese has melted, add the sunflower flour mixture and whisk to thoroughly blend the ingredients.
9. To create a smooth dough, properly combine the egg and salt.
10. Roll the dough into sticks after dividing it into equal halves.
11. Breadsticks should be placed in a single layer on a baking sheet greased with oil.
12. Create lines on the breadsticks using the back of a knife or a metal spoon.
13. When the breadsticks are golden brown, place the baking sheet on the grill and cook for 12 minutes.

14. After removing the baking sheet from the grill, give the breadsticks some time to cool.
15. Serve.

Nutrition: Carbohydrates: 0.6 g Protein: 1.2 g Cholesterol: 7 mg

Simple Roasted Butternut Squash

Ingredients:

◊ 2 garlic cloves (minced)
◊ 1 (2 pounds) butternut squash
◊ 2 tablespoons extra olive virgin oil
◊ Salt and pepper to taste
◊ 1 teaspoon oregano
◊ 1 teaspoon paprika
◊ 1 teaspoon thyme

PREPARATION:
5 MINUTES

COOKING TIME:
25 MINUTES

SERVINGS:
8

Directions:

1. Set your grill to the "smoke" setting and keep it open for 5 minutes or until it catches fire. A 400°F grill should be used.
2. Peel the butternut squash.
3. Butternut squash should be split in half (cut lengthwise).
4. Scoop out the seeds with a spoon.
5. Butternut squash should be cut into 1-inch cubes, then washed in water.
6. Chunks of butternut squash should be combined with the other ingredients in a large bowl.
7. Stir the mixture just long enough to coat the chunks.
8. On the sheet pan, distribute the coated pieces.
9. Bake the sheet pan for 25 minutes on the grill.
10. Butternut squash that has been baked should be taken off the heat and left to cool.
11. Serve.

Nutrition: Carbohydrates: 13.8 g Protein: 1.2 g Cholesterol: 0 mg

Empanadas

Ingredients:

◊ ½ teaspoon baking powder
◊ 3/4 cup + 1 tablespoon all-purpose flour
◊ 1 small beaten egg
◊ 1tablespoon sugar
◊ 2 tablespoons cold water
◊ ¼ teaspoon salt or to taste
◊ 1/3 cups butter

PREPARATION:
20 MINUTES

COOKING TIME:
20 MINUTES

FILLING:

◊ 57 g ground beef (1/8 pound)
◊ 1/2 teaspoon ground black pepper or to taste
◊ ½ chopped small onion
◊ 1 tablespoon olive oil
◊ 2 tablespoons marinara sauce
◊ 1/8 peeled and diced small potato (35 grams)
◊ 1 peeled and diced small carrot
◊ 2 tablespoons of water
◊ 1 minced garlic clove
◊ 1 tablespoon raisin
◊ 1 sliced hard-boiled egg
◊ ½ teaspoon salt or taste
◊ 2 tablespoons green peas

SERVINGS:
4

Directions:

1. Turn on the smoke on your grill and keep the lid open for five minutes or until the fire begins.
2. Using hickory hardwood pellets, seal the grill and heat it to 400°F for 15 minutes with the lid closed.

3. Place a cast iron pan with oil on the grill to prepare the fillet.

4. Add the garlic and the onions to the heated oil and cook until the onion is soft and transparent.

5. Add the ground beef and cook it, often turning, until it is soft.

6. Add the salt, pepper, and marinara after stirring.

7. Turn down the heat after bringing it to a boil. For 30 seconds, cook.

8. Cook for 3 minutes after stirring the potatoes, carrots, and raisins.

9. Add the sliced egg and green peas after mixing. Stirring often, cook for a further 2 minutes.

10. Apply non-stick spray to a baking pan.

11. In a sizable mixing basin, assemble the flour, salt, baking powder, and sugar to make the dough. Combine well after mixing.

12. When adding the butter, stir it in well.

13. The dough will form as you continue to stir in the egg.

14. The dough should be placed on a floured surface and worked for a few minutes. If the dough is not thick enough, add additional flour.

15. A rolling pin is used to flatten the dough. The dough should be 1/4 inch thick when it is flat.

16. Cut circles out of the flat dough.

17. Each flat circular dough should have equal quantities of the meat mixture in the center. The dough slice's edges are sealed by folding it over and pushing with your fingers or a fork.

18. Put the empanadas in a single layer on the baking sheet.

19. Bake the baking sheet for 10 minutes on the grill.

20. Flip the empanadas after removing the baking sheet from the grill.

21. Grill the empanadas for 10 minutes or until they are golden brown.

Nutrition: Carbohydrates: 28.9 g Protein: 10.4 g Cholesterol: 129 mg

Chapter 7
Desserts Recipes

Grilled Pound Cake with Fruit Dressing

Ingredients:

◊ 1/8 cup melted butter
◊ 1buttermilk pound cake, sliced into 3/4 inch slices
◊ 1/2 cup raspberries
◊ 1.1/2 cup whipped cream
◊ 1/2 cup blueberries
◊ 1/2 cup sliced strawberries

PREPARATION:
20 MINUTES

COOKING TIME:
50 MINUTES

SERVINGS:
12

Directions:

1. Preheat the pellet grill to 400 degrees. If appropriate, set your smoke setting to high.
2. Melted butter should be applied to each slice of pound cake on both sides.
3. Cook for 5 minutes on each side when placed directly on the grill grate. Turn the cake 90 degrees midway through cooking each side to create chequered grill markings.
4. If you desire deeper grill marks and a smokey taste, you may cook the food for a few more minutes.
5. Slices of pound cake should be taken from the grill and let cool on a dish.
6. Slices may be garnished as desired with raspberries, blueberries, whipped cream, and sliced strawberries. Distribute and savor!

Nutrition: Carbohydrates: 33.1 g Protein: 3.4 g Cholesterol: 64.7 mg

Smoked Pumpkin Pie

Ingredients:

◊ 1-1/2 tablespoon pumpkin pie spice
◊ 1 unbaked pie shell
◊ 1 tablespoon cinnamon
◊ 15 oz. can of pumpkin
◊ 2 beaten eggs
◊ 14 oz. can of sweetened condensed milk
◊ Topping: whipped cream

PREPARATION:
10 MINUTES

COOKING TIME:
50 MINUTES

SERVINGS:
8

Directions:

1. Set your grill to 325 °F.
2. Use a cake plate or a rimmed baking sheet to place upside down on the smoker.
3. Pour the batter into a pie crust after mixing all ingredients in a large basin apart from the pie shell.
4. Put the pie on the baking sheet and bake for 50 to 60 minutes, or until a knife comes out clean when inserted into its center. Ensure the center is set.
5. Remove and let cool for two hours or place in the fridge overnight.
6. Enjoy it while being served with whipped cream on top!

Nutrition: Carbohydrates: 40 g Protein: 7 g Cholesterol: 292 mg

Grilled Fruit and Cream

Ingredients:

◊ 1 halved nectarine
◊ 2 halved apricots
◊ 2 halved peaches
◊ ½ cup balsamic vinegar
◊ ½ cup raspberries
◊ ¼ cup blueberries
◊ 2 tablespoons honey
◊ 2 cups of cream
◊ 1 orange, peel

PREPARATION:
15 MINUTES

COOKING TIME:
10 MINUTES

SERVINGS:
4

Directions:

1. Set your smoker to 400°F with the lid closed.
2. For four minutes on each side, grill nectarines, peaches, and apricots.
3. Set a pan on the stovetop and adjust the heat to medium.
4. Add 2 teaspoons each of vinegar, honey, and orange peel.
5. Simmer until it gets medium-thick
6. Cream and honey should be combined in a bowl and whipped until soft.
7. Place the berries, fruits, and balsamic reduction on the serving platter.
8. Enjoy your dish with cream!

Nutrition: Carbohydrates: 35 g Protein: 34 g Cholesterol: 62 mg

Pellet Grill Apple Crisp

Ingredients:

◊ 10 large apples
◊ Apples
◊ 3 cups oatmeal, old-fashioned
◊ 1/2 cup flour
◊ 1/2 tablespoon cinnamon
◊ 2 cups brown sugar
◊ 1 cup sugar, dark brown
◊ 1/2 cup butter slices
◊ 1-1/2 cups softened butter, salted
◊ Crisp
◊ 1-1/2 tablespoon cinnamon

PREPARATION:
20 MINUTES

COOKING TIME:
1 HOURS

SERVINGS:
15

Directions:

1. Set your grill to 350 degrees.
2. Apples should be cleaned, peeled, cored, and diced into medium-sized chunks.
3. Combine dark brown sugar, cinnamon, and flour before adding apple chunks.
4. After using cooking spray to coat the baking pan (10x13), add the apples. Add slices of butter on top.
5. In a medium bowl, thoroughly mix all the ingredients for the crisp. Over the apples, spread the mixture.
6. Place on the grill and cook for approximately an hour to ensure the cooking is even every 15 to 20 minutes. Never put it on the hottest portion of the grill.
7. Remove and let settle for around 20-25 minutes
8. Enjoy.

Nutrition: Carbohydrates: 70 g Protein: 4 g Cholesterol: 528 mg

Pellet Grill Chocolate Chip Cookies

Ingredients:

◊ 1 cup of sugar
◊ 1 cup softened salted butter
◊ 1 cup light brown sugar
◊ 2 large eggs
◊ 2 teaspoon vanilla extract
◊ 3 cups all-purpose flour
◊ 1/2 teaspoon baking powder
◊ 1 teaspoon baking soda
◊ 2 cups semi-sweet chocolate chunks or chips
◊ 1 teaspoon natural sea salt

PREPARATION:
20 MINUTES

COOKING TIME:
45 MINUTES

SERVINGS:
12

Directions:

1. To 375°F, heat the pellet grill.
2. Put parchment paper on a large baking sheet and put it aside.
3. Mix the flour, baking soda, salt, and baking powder in a medium bowl. After mixing, put aside.
4. Combine the white sugar, butter, and brown sugar in the bowl of a stand mixer. Beat the vanilla and eggs after mixing till fluffy.
5. Add the dry ingredients and whisk everything together.
6. Add the chocolate chips and combine well.
7. At a time, form three tablespoons of dough into balls and set them on the cookie sheet. Place them evenly apart, with two to three inches between each ball.
8. Bake the cookies for 20 to 25 minutes, or until the outsides are just beginning to brown. Place cookie sheet immediately on the grill grate.
9. Take off the grill and let the food sit for 10 minutes. Distribute and savor!

Nutrition: Carbohydrates: 22.8 g Protein: 1.4 g Cholesterol: 7.8 mg

Nectarine and Nutella Sundae

Ingredients:

◊ 2 teaspoon honey
◊ 2 halved and pitted nectarines
◊ 4 tablespoons of Nutella
◊ 4 cherries to top
◊ 1/4 cup chopped pecans
◊ 4 scoops of vanilla ice cream
◊ Whipped cream to top

PREPARATION:
10 MINUTES

COOKING TIME:
25 MINUTES

SERVINGS:
4

Directions:

1. Preheat the pellet grill to 400 degrees.
2. Nectarines should be pitted and cut in half.
3. Apply honey on the cut side (inside) of each nectarine half.
4. Nectarines should be placed cut side down immediately on the grill grate. Grill marks should appear after 5 to 6 minutes of cooking.
5. Cook nectarines for two minutes on the other side after flipping.
6. Nectarines should be taken from the grill and let cool.
7. A tablespoon of Nutella should be placed in each nectarine half's pit cavity.
8. On top of the Nutella, place 1 scoop of ice cream. For toppings, add cherries, whipping cream, and chopped pecans. Distribute and savor!

Nutrition: Carbohydrates: 15 g Protein: 2 g Cholesterol: 0 mg

Grilled Peaches and Cream

Preparation Time: 15 minutes

Cooking Time: 8 minutes

Servings: 8

Ingredients:

◊   1 cup cream cheese, soft with nuts and honey

◊   1 tablespoon vegetable oil

◊   4 halved and pitted peaches

◊   2 tablespoons clover honey

**PREPARATION:
15 MINUTES**

**COOKING TIME:
8 MINUTES**

**SERVINGS:
8**

Directions:

1. Set the temperature on your pellet grill to medium-high.

2. After giving them a thin oil coating, place the peaches on the grill pit side.

3. Grill for approximately 5 minutes or until the surfaces have lovely grill marks.

4. After turning the peaches over, sprinkle honey over them.

5. Spread the filling evenly, dot some cream cheese on top, and cook for an additional two to three minutes, or until the filling is warm.

6. Serve right away.

Nutrition: Carbohydrates: 11.6 g Protein: 1.1 g Cholesterol: 139 mg

Conclusion

Nowadays, there are many possibilities when it comes to grilling. One of the most used grilling methods is the use of pellets. They are simple to use with a variety of simple setup and use capabilities. Grills made of pellets heat up faster than grills made of conventional charcoal. The burning pellet woods provide a delightful smokey taste and stable heat when grilling fish, meat, or vegetables. The wood pellets burn cleanly and produce very little ash since they are additive-free.

In conclusion, pellet grills and smokers provide an alluring blend of user-friendly features and culinary variety. After placing your food, adjusting the temperature, and feeding the pellet hopper, you hardly need to touch them.

They are capable of cooking nearly anything, and they will provide an authentic smoky taste to slow-cooked meat. Some people use it as their go-to grill for all of their outdoor cooking. However, it isn't excellent enough for grilling or smoking to justify the cost for other people. If you fall into this category, spending your money on distinct, task-specific units could be wiser.

Made in the USA
Monee, IL
27 December 2023